Lessons to be Learned: A Study of Eighteenth Century English Didactic Children's Literature

American University Studies

Series XIV
Education

Vol. 7

PETER LANG
New York · Berne · Frankfurt am Main

Bette P. Goldstone

Lessons to be Learned
A Study of Eighteenth Century English Didactic Children's Literature

PETER LANG
New York · Berne · Frankfurt am Main

Library of Congress Cataloging in Publication Data

Goldstone, Bette P., 1947–
  Lessons to be Learned.

  (American University Studies. Series XIV, Education;
vol. 7)
  Bibliography: p.
  1. English Literature – 18th Century – History and
Criticism. 2. Didactic Literature, English – History and
Criticism. 3. Children's Literature, English – History
and Criticism. 4. Children – Great Britain – Books and
Reading. I. Title. II. Series.
  PR448.D53G65 1984   820'.9'9287   84-47785
  ISBN 0-8204-0140-4
  ISSN 0740-4565

CIP-Kurztitelaufnahme der Deutschen Bibliothek

Goldstone, Bette P.:
Lessons to be Learned: A Study of Eighteenth
Century English Didact. Children's Literature /
Bette P. Goldstone. – New York; Berne;
Frankfurt am Main: Lang, 1984.
  (American University Studies: Ser. 14,
  Education; Vol. 7)
  ISBN 0-8204-0140-4

NE: American University Studies / 14

© Peter Lang Publishing, Inc., New York 1984

Printed by Lang Druck, Inc., Liebefeld/Berne (Switzerland)

Dedicated to

P.K.P., a most charming bibliophile

and to Avra and Rebecca

TABLE OF CONTENTS

PREFACE

I became interested in eighteenth century English didactic children's literature when I was teaching a children's literature course at Temple University in Philadelphia. Early in the semester, a lecture or two would be devoted to the history of juvenile books. After reviewing the important books of the pre-Newbery era, and then discussing Newbery and his renowned publications, an overview of the British didactic school would begin, including such notable members of the group as Mrs. Barbauld, Mrs. Trimmer, Maria Edgeworth, Mary Jane Kilner and Dorothy Kilner. As I read brief selections from Maria Edgeworth's "Rosamond and the Purple Jar" and Mrs. Trimmer's Fabulous Histories, the class would titter as they listened to the stilted language and heavy moral overtones. With relief, we left this seemingly sullen, lifeless period to enter the beautiful world of Victorian children's literature.

Although I too was bemused while reading aloud these late eighteenth century didactic selections, I was also intrigued by them. My cursory reading of commentary on that particular time period certainly supported the class's general opinion that it was dull, antiquated stuff. Yet I actually enjoyed them. I began to read the stories in their entirety and found that I was charmed by the tales. I also was left after reading them, with a feeling of reassurance: I was reassured of the dignity of man, hope for the future, and a promise that good for the most part will triumph over evil. True, the moral messages lay

heavily on the page, true the books were filled with tedious
"teaching lessons"; still these books seemed to have something
more, something special.

A personal incident further piqued my interest in these
didactic writings. Upon returning home after reading Maria
Edgeworth's Parent's Assistant, I found myself cleaning my
kitchen cabinets. Upon self examination (for this is not a
common mode of behavior for me), I felt certain that it was
Simple Susan, a twelve year old character created by Miss Edgeworth, who had motived this domestic activity. Susan was a
child of sweet and patient disposition who managed to raise
money to pay off her father's debt, keep an immaculate house,
nurse her ailing mother, teach her younger siblings their
ABC's, and take charge of the village children while they were
at play. If, at such a tender age, she was able to accomplish
so much, certainly I as an adult, could straighten out my
rather messy kitchen cupboards. What struck me about this incident was if I, not being of an age that is considered "impressionable," was so moved to action by this little story, how
many before me had been prompted to emulate behaviors and
morals from these writings?

Therefore, with interest aroused, I began to study late
eighteenth century British didactic children's literature.
This manuscript is the product of that research. I sincerely
hope that it helps to vindicate the authors and the books of
this time period from the ostensibly negative criticism they
have received in the past fifty years.

CHAPTER I

INTRODUCTION

Need for the Study

Children's literature is a relatively new phenomenon in the history of literature. Although there have been manner books and school texts produced since the Middle Ages, it was not until the late seventeenth century when stories written specifically for children appeared in any significant amount. John Newbery in the mid-eighteenth century, probably more from the vantage of the entrepreneur than out of an altruistic concern for children, was the first who truly organized and proliferated the concept of literature for the young. His Pretty Little Pocket Book and Goody Two Shoes, as well as his other publications caught the imagination of the young, and more importantly legitimized the concept of writing fiction for the young in a format and style that was particularly suited for them. There is no question that Newbery's genius and foresight were unique and many researchers feel that children's literature did not again reach the quality of his books until the Victorian era.

The children's literature that followed in England in the second half of the eighteenth century is generally called the didactic school. Written ostensibly by women, often mothers and aunts creating tales for their own relatives, these authors followed many of John Newbery's innovative ideas. What marked these writers apart from others was their firm belief that literature presented to the young should be, in fact, lessons, prettily written of course, but nevertheless they should very specifically teach the child about the moral and ethical issues of the day.

Today, these late eighteenth century stories are classified as "forgotten books." The artificiality of language, the quaint presentations of manners, and the overwhelming didactic style have caused these books to disappear from the rank and file of juvenile library collections. Until quite recently, except for collectors with rare insight, they were discarded or left decaying in library basements. Now, because of their monetary value and the renewed interest in historical children's books, they are housed in rare book collections. At times, their text is placed on microfilm, to insure that no further harm comes to their precious if not precarious state. Despite their value and the care lavished upon them, they are still considered oddities-- brief glimpses of the past, certainly not quality literature. When these didactic books are discussed in twentieth century texts, they are often negatively reviewed and cited as examples of what children's literature should not be.

One has to question both the lack of interest and negative reviews given to a group of books that captivated (or at least were reprinted for) a juvenile audience for fifty, one hundred and sometimes one hundred and fifty years. It also seems odd that so little importance is given to a group of books that should hold a definite place in the development of children's literature. If John Newbery is considered the father of children's literature, as we know it today, it then seems important to study and understand the children's books that immediately followed his publications. The writers of these late eighteenth century books helped to keep alive this new genre--literature for the young. Also, when time is taken to critically read these didactic children's books, one can find charming, well written passages, a foreshadowing of the brilliance that will emerge in the great Victorian juvenile literature and the Golden Age of the early twentieth century.

It therefore seems both appropriate and relevant to critically re-examine some of the late eighteenth century British didactic children's literature and give these books the just notice they deserve.

Delineation of the Study

The five juvenile fiction books selected for this study are Evenings at Home (1792-1796) by Mrs. Barbauld and Dr. Aiken; Fabulous Histories (1786) by Mrs. Trimmer; The Parent's Assistant (1796) by Maria Edgeworth; The Life and Perambulations of a Mouse (1783?) by Dorothy Kilner; and Jemima Placid (1785?) by Mary Jane Kilner. The rationale for selection is as follows:

1) According to histories of children's literature, these books are representative of late eighteenth century didactic children's literature.

2) They are frequently cited in nineteenth and twentieth

century commentaries on children's literature.

3) They have secular themes.

4) They had considerably long life spans, going through
many reprintings.

5) They were, according to nineteenth century reviewers,
enjoyed by their young readers.

6) The authors of these books were influential in their
day, having an impact on contemporary educational theories
and/or other writers for children.

7) The authors of these books thought of themselves primarily as writers of children's literature. (For this reason,
Sandford and Merton has been excluded from this study. The
author, Thomas Day, considered himself an educational theorist,
specifically disseminating the principles of Rousseau.) This
point is significant because the authors of earlier children's
books considered themselves not as writers for children, but
rather as publishers (Newbery, et al.), educational theorists
(Comenius, et al.), evangelists (Bunyan, et al.), or penned the
children's book as just a minor writing aspect of their writing
careers (Oliver Goldsmith, et al.).

Organization of the Study

This manuscript has been constructed to give a totality of
impression: a picture of the social and historical trends occur-
ring when these books were written, biographical data on the
authors, documentary evidence indicating the marketability of
the selected books, and critical book reviews. The inclusion of

this related information is necessary, otherwise, as Elizabeth Nesbitt suggested, historical books do not receive just apprais- al.[1] Peter Opie further commented that children's literature is far too often "separated from the times and conditions in which it was produced; in short that we are beginning not only to be unable to see the wood for the trees, but unable to see even the ground in which the trees have roots."[2] Therefore, the first major section includes a review of the historical trends of the eighteenth century--the social, political, and economic forces that helped shape the thinking of the authors, and influenced their writing. In evaluating books of any sort, Paul Heins wrote that the trends of an age must be considered.[3] Biographi- cal information on the authors will also be given. Not only were the authors influential and fascinating personalities, it is also important to be familiar with the personal history of an author, for memories are "called up consciously and unconscious- ly" when the author writes.[4]

To understand children's literature, one must also under- stand the child for which it is written. Therefore, a discussion of prevalent childrearing practices and the conceptualization of

---

[1]Sara Innis Fenwick, ed., A Critical Approach to Children's Literature (Chicago: University of Chicago, 1967), p. 125.

[2]Peter Opie, "John Newbery and His Successors," Book Col- lector, 24 (Summer 1975), pp. 263, 264.

[3]Virginia Haviland, ed., Children and Literature: Views and Reviews (New York: Lothrop, Lee and Shepard, 1973), p. 410.

[4]Katherine Paterson, "Sounds in the Heart," The Horn Book, 6 (December 1981), p. 695.

childhood is included. There is an attitude among reviewers
that childhood has an "unchanging quality."[5] Recent studies of
the history of childhood have proven this just is not so. The
conceptualization of the child in the fourteenth century was
vastly different from the eighteenth century's. This conceptualization is markedly different from our own modern view of
children. It is the adult's conceptualization of the child that
determines child rearing practices--the child is molded socially
and intellectually accordingly. Our children today would have a
difficult time playing with a child of the late eighteenth century. They simply are different. Their contrasting attitudes
about the world, about themselves, about social mores would push
them apart. The literature that the eighteenth century child
enjoyed could very well be considerably different from the literature that our children today cherish.

The second research section will try to ascertain if these
eighteenth century didactic books were actually read and enjoyed
by children. To do this, there is a two part analysis. The
first includes eyewitness reports; commentary of persons who had
read the selected books as children, statements made by children
themselves, and reviews by contemporary and near contemporary
literary critics. The second is a study of the documentary reprinting evidence found in the National Union Catalogue. A list
of the reprintings is given, and the data is investigated in
terms of:

---

[5]Doris M. Cole, ed., The Reading of Children: A Symposium
(Syracuse: Syracuse University, 1964), p. 22.

(1) Life spans of the books;

(2) Reprintings within the first years of publication;

(3) Geographical distribution;

(4) The number of publishing houses involved;

(5) The illustrators/engravers commissioned.

It is demonstrated in this section that prominent illustrators and publishing firms became involved with these books. Certainly they would not risk damaging their reputations by involving themselves with books that would not sell or with authors who were not respectable. The selected five books were published in several cities spanning two continents showing that the buying market had a wider geographical distribution than just the environs of London. The books also had considerably long life spans. Some even competed with children's books written in the late nineteenth and early twentieth centuries; books, both in terms of literary quality and imagination, that are far superior to the eighteenth century didactic writings. The multiple reprintings in their early years of publication is also an indication of immediate popularity.

The last research section is a critical evaluation of the books themselves. The traditional criteria of style (the formation of the writing which expresses the individuality and intent of the author), theme (the central concept of a literary work), plot (a series of author-planned actions moving to a meaningful conclusion), and characterization (description of an imaginary person)[6] is used in the evaluation. Also included

---

[6]The definitions of style, plot, theme, and characteriza-

are relevant interpretative commentary and appropriate selections from the books themselves, for the review should "create
the spirit and essence of the book, not merely the plot,"[7] by
adding "intellectual and emotional analysis."[8]

Review of the Literature

In general, the didactic children's literature of the late
eighteenth century is negatively reviewed by modern historians
and commentators of children's literature. James Steele Smith
summed up the critics by writing, "most of us find this sort of
writing for children amazing, unbelievable--in short, silly or
ridiculous."[9] Monica Kiefer noted that the eighteenth century
didactic authors' philosophy and writing destroyed the sense of
fantasy and make believe in children's books.[10] Lillian Smith
stated that with the "coming of the later half of the eighteenth century, the Age of Reason began, the door to imagination
was shut." She continued by writing that "none of these
strongly didactic books for children have survived except as

---

tion were adapted from William Thrall and Addison Hubbard, A
Handbook of Literature, revised by C. Hugh Holman (New York:
The Odyssey Press, 1960).

[7]Fenwick, A Critical Approach to Children's Literature, p.
125.

[8]Ibid., p. 122.

[9]James Steele Smith, A Critical Approach to Children's
Literature (New York: McGraw-Hill, 1967), p. 48.

[10]Monica Kiefer, American Children Through their Books:
1700-1835 (Philadelphia: University of Pennsylvania, 1948), p.
18.

curiosities, since the authors ignore the nature, the environment and the inclination of the children for whom they wrote."[11]
The authors of A Critical History of Children's Literature con-
tended that these didactic books lacked sympathy for the child
and the gaiety that he needed.[12] They were "devoid of style"
wrote Isabelle Jan, "They contain no plot and are only show-
cases for social mores."[13] She also criticized their stiff
dialogue.[14] Targ in Bibliophile in the Nursery described the
characters as "impossible children and perfect parents."[15]

In the classic Children's Books in England, F. J. Harvey
Darton likened the characters in the didactic tales to the
"brats of the movable-head books: the same waxen face fitted
into a succession of stiff bodies."[16] Paul Hazard also criticized their style by saying specifically that Mrs. Trimmer's
writing was "odious to read and her wordy writing bore us to
death." Maria Edgeworth was "useless in mixing instruction

---

[11]Lillian Smith, The Unreluctant Years (New York: The
Viking Press, 1953), p. 25.

[12]Cornelia Meigs, Elizabeth Nesbitt, Anne Thaxter Eaton,
Ruth Hill Viquers, A Critical History of Children's Literature
(New York: Macmillan, 1967), p. 63.

[13]Isabelle Jan, On Children's Literature (London: Bayles
and Sons, Ltd., 1973), p. 23.

[14]Ibid., p. 22.

[15]William Targ, ed., Bibliophile in the Nursery (New York:
The World Publishing Co., 1957), p. 335.

[16]F. J. Harvey Darton, Children's Books in England: Five
Centuries of Social Life (Cambridge: Cambridge University
Press, 1958), p. 169.

with amusement." Mrs. Barbauld was equally "fearsome."[17]
Alice Dalgliesh accused the didactic writers of being Puritanical in outlook and whose books were failures in terms of literary worth[18] and in reforming the manners of the young.[19]
Annie Moore wrote that "didacticism, condescension, and propa-
ganda are the natural enemies of the reading habit of children."[20] These books cultivated a "premature self-consciousness
on the part of the child."[21] Percy Muir lambasted the authors
by referring to them as "The Monstrous Regiment."[22] The eminent Oxford philosopher, J. H. Plumb, suggested that the didactic eighteenth century authors were anachronistic, reintroduc-
ing Calvinistic views of childhood.[23] He also questioned if
these didactic books were even read by children.[24] In Literature and the Child, one of the newest texts in the field, the
discussion of the eighteenth century didactic writing is not

---

[17]Paul Hazard, Books, Children and Men (Boston: The Horn
Book, Inc., 1947), p. 37.

[18]Alice Dalgliesh, First Experiences with Literature (New
York: Charles Scribner's Sons, 1932), p. ix.

[19]Ibid., p. x.

[20]Annie E. Moore, Literature Old and New for Children
(Cambridge, Massachusetts: Houghton Mifflin, 1934), p. 50.

[21]Ibid., p. 184.

[22]Percy Muir, English Books from 1600-1900 (New York:
Frederick A. Praeger, 1934), p. 82.

[23]J. H. Plumb, "The New World of Children in Eighteenth-
Century England," Past and Present, 67 (1975): 91.

[24]J. H. Plumb, Introduction to Early Children's Books and
the Illustration (Boston: David R. Godine, 1975), p. xxii.

only quite brief, but also negative in tone.[25]

These twentieth century commentators criticized the style, characterization, plot, theme, and general readability of these books and found fault with the authors for being insensitive to their young readers' psyches and interests. At times, they questioned whether these books should even be classified as children's books. Rather, some researchers suggested that they were exercises on the part of a group of women to elevate themselves as educational theorists[26] or to write books that would gain the approval of the adult generation.[27] If these statements are correct, then what accounts for the many reprintings of these books and the positive reviews they received throughout the nineteenth and early twentieth century?

Mrs. Trimmer's Fabulous Histories (1786) was reprinted in the twentieth century. Bertha Mahoney noted in Realms of Gold that Maria Edgeworth's stories were being read and enjoyed through the 1920's.[28] In Andrew Tuer's Pages and Pictures of Forgotten Children's Books (1898-99), it is interesting to note that Fabulous Histories, Maria Edgeworth's tales and Mrs. Barbauld's work are most noticeably missing. Could this be interpreted as not being an oversight on the part of the author but

[25] Bernice E. Cullinan, Literature and the Child (New York: Harcourt Brace Jovanovich, 1981), p. 46.

[26] Targ, Bibliophile in the Nursery, p. 335.

[27] Plumb, Introduction to Early Children's Books, p. xxii.

[28] Bertha Mahoney, ed., Realms of Gold in Children's Books (New York: Doubleday, Dorant and Co., 1929), p. 614.

rather that they were not, at that time, "forgotten"? McGuffy's Readers, in its attempt to compile high quality, appealing, and appropriate reading for the young, included one of Maria Edgeworth's stories in its 1909 edition. The books of the Kilner sisters were being published in the nineteenth century.

Mrs. Barbauld's Evenings at Home was reprinted up to the first decade of the twentieth century. One cannot dismiss the long life of these tales simply by assuming that they were bought by adoring aunts and grandmamas to lay on the nursery shelves gathering dust. Nor is it correct to suggest that these books were read simply because there was a dearth of literature for the young. Contrary to the common belief that there were few books written for children in this time period, the eighteenth century produced a veritable onslaught of children's literature--school texts, religious tractates, poetry, and many novels geared to both children as well as to the young adult audience. Mrs. Sarah Trimmer reviewed hundreds of children's books in her five volume Guardian of Education (1802-1806), and obviously she did not critique every book available. A lack of reading material does not seem to be the issue.

Nineteenth century reviewers and historians of children's literature seem to present a much more positive view of these didactic books, even though they were cognizant that these books were not classics. What is important is that they suggested that they were beloved by their readers and that these books were of some literary worth. In the classic 1844 article in Quarterly Review, considered to be the first true review of

children's literature, the anonymous author gave a list of
children's books that she deemed as quality literature. Mrs.
Trimmer's <u>Fabulous Histories</u>, Maria Edgeworth's <u>Parent's Assis-</u>
<u>tant</u>, and <u>Evenings at Home</u> were included.

In Miss Yonge's delightful article in <u>Macmillan's Magazine</u>
(1869), she wrote of Dorothy Kilner's book:

> The "Perambulations of a Mouse" was another favo-
> rite, in spite of language such as might be an-
> ticipated from that name . . . . There was an
> exceeding charm in the first start in life by the
> four brother mice, Nimble, Longtails, Brighteyes,
> and Softdown; and considerable pathos (at least
> in the infant mind) in the gradual diminution of
> the brotherhood, until Nimble remained to the
> last, alone to tell his tale. And the conversa-
> tions he overhears are related with such spirit,
> that one only longs to hear more of such inter-
> esting people.[29]

Of Mrs. Trimmer she wrote--"Her 'Fabulous Histories' have quite
another kind of charm: Robin, Dicky, Flapsy, and Pecksey, have
real character, quite enough to carry the reader over the long
words in which the parent robins, and their patrons indulge."[30]
Her comments on Mrs. Barbauld's <u>Evenings at Home</u> are the following: "and in looking back at these little performances we
are struck by the perfect precision and polish of language,
even of the most simple, such as renders them almost as complete epigrams as Aesoph's fables, and contrasts with the
slovenly writing of the present day."[31]

---

[29]Miss Yonge, "Children's Literature of the Last Century,"
<u>Macmillan's Magazine</u> (July 1869), p. 231.

[30]<u>Ibid</u>., p. 231.

[31]<u>Ibid</u>., p. 233.

In 1891, Charles Welsh, a well respected and frequently published historian of children's literature, wrote an article for the Newbery House Magazine. It was a brief history of children's literature in which he collected from contemporary luminaries recollections of their favorite childhood readings. Excerpts from some of these recollections are given below.

> A distinguished statesman, whose name I am not at liberty to use, writing of the books he read 60-70 years ago . . . I ought not to be unmindful of "Sanford and Merton"; "Evenings at Home" and above all I ought to notice the genuine stories of Miss Edgeworth, which, with all her faults, were dear to children. "Simple Susan" which Sir Walter Scott could sit down and cry over, was an attractive tale.[32]

The Bishop of Wakefield recollected in the article, "My fondness for 'Natural History,' as it would then be called, was stimulated by 'Evenings at Home,' which was certainly one of my chief favorites . . . as were Miss Edgeworth's tales . . . [and] Mrs. Trimmer's 'Robins' were very popular with us."[33] Walter Crane reminisced that "'Evenings at Home' was a favorite."[34]

Early histories of children's literature are also positive in their discussion of the didactic school. Two such texts are Mrs. Field's A Child and His Book (1892) and Florence Barry's A Century of Children's Books (1922). Both authors review the children's books that preceded their time, paying special attention to the literature in the second half of the eighteenth

---

[32] Charles Welsh, "Some Notes on the History of Children's Books," Newbery House Magazine (February 1891), p. 216.

[33] Ibid., p. 217.

[34] Ibid., p. 220.

century. In Mrs. Field's chapter "To Point a Moral, and Adorn a Tale" she wrote of the didactic eighteenth century children's books that "The moral then was the keynote, but the merit of the works produced varies immensely. In looking at a batch of them, we find some in which a writer of real talent has clothed the dry bones of morality with living flesh and blood."[35] One example of a book that goes beyond the telling of moral platitudes, she wrote, was Evenings at Home. The author stated,

> Mrs. Barbauld is perhaps best remembered now as the joint author with her brother of "Evenings at Home." We need hardly say more of this book here; it is evergreen in the memory of my own generation and it is perhaps not too much to say that any child of any generation would equally appreciate it. Recent reprints will at least give the opportunity to the present race of children. [36]

Mrs. Field applauded Mrs. Trimmer by writing that "the delightful 'Fabulous Histories' now generally known as 'The History of the Robins,' which has been continually reprinted, though subjected to an amount of editing which seems sufficiently uncalled for and impertinent to those who loved the book in its old form."[37] Mrs. Field was aware of the negative criticism given to the eighteenth century didactic writings. Her feelings about these criticisms were shown in her comments about Maria Edgeworth's Parent's Assistant. "Perhaps it is well to avoid bringing too much destructive criticism to bear

---

[35] Mrs. Field, The Child and His Book (London: Wells, Gardner, Darton and Co., 1892), pp. 249-250.

[36] Ibid., p. 263.

[37] Ibid., p. 267.

upon the morality held up to admiration . . . . We may as well shut our eyes to either sort of error, and take the stories as stories, and right good ones."[38]

Florence Barry, whose work is highly regarded and was often referred to in Darton's classic history of children's literature, devoted five chapters to the discussion of the didactic children's writers of the later half of the eighteenth century. She, like Mrs. Field, was aware of the flaws found in these books, but for the most part treated these writings in a positive light. For example, she quoted the following ditty written about Dorothy Kilner:

> Chief of our Aunts--not only I
> But all your dozen of nurslings cry--
> What did other children do
> And what were Childhood, wanting you?[39]

Her comments on Mrs. Trimmer were:

> The Robin family is more than half human. Nest-
> lings, distinguished by the expressive names of
> Robin, Dicky, Flapsy and Pecksey, exhibit all the
> faults of children, but there is a world of dif-
> ference between Mrs. Trimmer's treatment and that
> of a fabulist. She has learned to look at a nest
> of birds from a child's point of view; what is
> infinitely more novel and surprising, she actu-
> ally shifts her ground and considers the Benson
> household from the standpoint of a bird. It is
> here that so many of her imitators lost the
> trail; and thus it is that their books were soon
> forgotten, while hers was read with delight for a
> century.[40]

She realistically appraised Mrs. Barbauld's work by writing:

---

[38]Ibid., pp. 270-271.

[39]Florence Barry, <u>A Century of Children's Books</u> (London: Methuen and Co., Ltd., 1922), p. 129.

[40]Ibid., pp. 137-138.

> It is true that none of Mrs. Barbauld's stories
> show [a] spirit of mischief. She was playful
> only in light verse or talk or letters; but she
> made her personality felt in a romantic attitude
> to life and Nature, which although it did not
> much affect her choice of subjects made her style
> unusually free and moving.[41]

Mrs. Barry recognized the importance of Maria Edgeworth to such
an extent that she devoted an entire chapter to her.

These nineteenth century historians and reviewers just
cited and Florence Barry, in the early twentieth century, were
able to put the late eighteenth century didactic children's
books in perspective. Although they recognized that these
books could not be considered children's literature classics,
they nevertheless knew that these books were enjoyed by children, and were often well written with the inclusion of novel
literary devices. These early reviewers gave the didactic
writings legitimacy as children's books and recognized their
position historically in the development of children's literature.[42] The twentieth century reviewers quoted, who took a
bleak if not antagonistic stance in regard to this eighteenth
century didactic literature, seem to be limited in their point
of view. They do not recognize the research and the nineteenth
century reviews that preceded them, the many reprintings of
these books, and are judging the books in terms of twentieth
century children's interests. They are not putting these early

---

[41]Ibid., pp. 148-149.

[42]This is not to say that negative criticism of these didactic writers did not exist earlier. At the turn of the nineteenth century, Charles Lamb and Wordsworth cleverly wrote
rather nasty comments about the contemporary didactic children's literature. Moore, Literature Old and New, pp. 209-210.

children's books in historical perspective.[43]

Although not classics, the five selected late eighteenth century British didactic books are important. They are an integral part in the history of children's literature for helping to define the newly emerging literary form--the children's novel. They deserve praise for the fact that they gave children reading pleasure for many, many years. This manuscript is an earnest effort to give this didactic literature the just notice it deserves.

---

[43]It should be noted that the shift from positive to negative criticism of eighteenth century didactic children's literature is strongly seen in the commentaries written from the mid-1920's to the mid-1930's. Whether this is a reflection of a change in educational or philosophical theories, or some other factor, deserves further consideration.

CHAPTER II

THE EIGHTEENTH CENTURY IN BRITAIN:
ATTITUDES, EVENTS, AND SELECTED BIOGRAPHIES

Introduction

Eighteenth century England was marred by no wars on its
soil, no class struggles, no sweeping political changes, no
momentous transformations in the church. Yet, it was a time
characterized by enormous change and growth. The economy was
slowly being changed by the inventions and improvements of the
pre-industrial and agricultural revolutions. The country was
prosperous, growing in population and was developing a belief
in its own ability to overcome obstacles. Scientific explora-
tions led to better medical care. The growth of humanitarian
activities created foundling hospitals for orphans and homes
for the poor. Roads were improved, the police force was reor-
ganized to increase effectiveness, a sanitation system was developed, and urban inhabitants now had fresh drinking water.
It was also a time marked by introspection, religious revival,
growing conservatism, and continued social injustice. The
agricultural land changes left thousands homeless and desti-
tute. The city slums were growing, filled with the despair and
degradation that has always characterized such areas. The
rapid scientific explosion left some with an inner confusion, a
void of faith. Despite all the inventions, the innovations,

and improvements bettering the quality of life; change was considered suspect.

Mrs. Barbauld, Mrs. Trimmer, Maria Edgeworth, Mary Jane
Kilner and Dorthy Kilner, the children's authors to be studied,
were very much products of their time. They were serious in
their endeavors and wished their books not only to be enjoyable
but also to show the children the accepted modes of behavior.
These authors wanted their books to actively help the young become useful and contented members of the society. Many of
their goals were structured by contemporary social thought.
Therefore, when trying to fully comprehend historical children's books, it is important to understand the times in which
they were written, the attitudes and mores which affected the
authors. Such understanding allows us to obtain a fuller sense
of the books themselves.

An Overview of the Social-Historical Trends

The eighteenth century in England is said to have truly
begun with the death of the last of the Stuarts, Queen Anne,
and the ascension of the Hanoverian, George I. King George was
fortunate to rule when the country was in relative calm. The
attitudes, mores, and social positions were very clearly defined in the first half of the 1700's. Major aspects of life
were thought to be pre-ordained, therefore accepted without
question. Society was controlled by what Samuel Johnson called
"the fixed, invariable, external rules of distinction of rank,"

a universal hierarchy entitled the "Scale of Being."[1] Those of
the lower classes were "appointed" to their life of poverty and
drudgery. Those more fortunate to be "appointed" into wealth
and rank, reaped the benefits from those beneath them. In return they governed the land wisely sometimes and at other times
not. All members of society understood and accepted unques-
tioningly their social status and the rules that accompanied
it. Pope, the poet laureate of the era, summed up the spirit of
the times when he wrote "Whatever Is . . . Is Right."[2] This
was an age characterized by contrived rationality, restraint,
and avoidance of extremes. Any form of enthusiasm was suspect
and "imagination was subordinated to good sense."[3]

Despite this philosophy of reason and rationality, despite
the ardent belief that the divinely organized class structure
was unshakeable, whatever was, was not always right. The first
half of the eighteenth century displayed a depravity and decadence that had not been seen since the days of Nero.[4] Gambling
reached epidemic proportions among the leisured classes. Fashionable clubs such as Almack's, White's and Boodle's drew men

---

[1]David Snoden, A Mighty Ferment: Britain in the Age of
Revolution 1750-1850 (New York: The Seabury Press, 1978), p.
10.

[2]Daniel Fader and George Bernstein, British Periodicals of
the Eighteenth and Nineteenth Centuries (Ann Arbor: University
Microfilms, 1972), p. 2.

[3]F. E. Halliway, An Illustrated Cultural History of England (New York: Viking Press, 1967), p. 193.

[4]John Gloag and C. Thompson Walter, Home Life in History:
Social Life and Manners in Britain: 200 B.C. - 1926 A.D. (New
York: Benjamin Blom, Inc., 1972), p. 235.

around the gaming tables hour after hour. Thousands of pounds
were wagered and lost. One Charles Fox had reportedly squan-
dered 140,000 pounds at cards by his twenty-fifth birthday.
The women, acting more discreetly of course, engaged in similar
pursuits in the privacy of their own drawing rooms.[5]

The drinking of gin, beer, port, and spirits, domestic and
imported, was excessive. Spirit bars boasted signboards which
coaxed customers to be "drunk for one penny, dead drunk for two
pence." Debauchers then were kindly invited to sleep off the
night's revelry on "straw for nothing."[6] This imbibing of al-
coholic beverages in huge quantities was not just part of the
upper classes' leisure time pursuits, or relegated to the lower
stratum of society. Johnson wrote that in his youth "all the
decent people in Lichfield got drunk every night, and were not
the worse thought of."[7] Brutal sports such as bear-baiting,
bull-baiting, and cock-fighting were the amusements enjoyed by
rich and poor alike.[8] The theater of the Restoration Drama,
and the early novel forms of Defoe and Fielding, display a
coarseness that even by today's standards would raise an eye-
brow or two.[9] Theft, street assaults, highway robbery, and

---

[5]A. S. Turberville, Men and Manners in the Eighteenth Century (Oxford: Clarendon Press, 1932), p. 85.

[6]Gloag and Walter, Home Life in History, p. 237.

[7]Turberville, Men and Manners in the Eighteenth Century,
p. 88.

[8]Ibid., p. 7.

[9]Ibid., p. 6.

shoplifting were daily occurrences.[10] Street gangs formed,
like the infamous Mohawks, whose members sallied forth at
night, drunk and armed, ready to inflict injury and outrage upon
innocent wayfarers.[11] Incongruous as it may seem, above this
brutality, a veneer of almost preposterous elegance and manner
was maintained. Formal bows, extended flowery expressions of
courtesy, and a pseudo-genteel mincing gait were the prescribed
code of fashion. Yet at the same time it was within the realm
of propriety for a gentleman to be drunk and foul-mouthed in
conversation with ladies.[12]

This debaucherous behavior of the upper classes was made,
if possible, even more offensive by a smugness of attitude.
Since theirs was a lot pre-ordained, nothing they believed,
could weaken or destroy their social position. Work was
shunned, leisure was pursued, and those not born to a high
social station were ignored--except when they were needed to
cook, clean, or labor. The rampant disease, the filth laden
streets, the wretched conditions of the poor went unnoticed.
By the mid part of the century, the moral situation was extremely low. In Toynbee's terms, the "creative minority," i.e.,
the upper classes, were losing their creativity and their
charm. There was a stagnation of the upper classes that could

---

[10]Gloag and Walter, Home Life in History, p. 238.

[11]Turberville, Men and Manners in the Eighteenth Century,
p. 84.

[12]Ibid., p. 98.

not be disputed.[13]

The picture thus far presented is bleak and could not have produced the moralistic, didactic literature of the late eighteenth century, if there had not been other social, scientific, and/or humanitarian attitudes emerging. The brutality and coarseness are undeniable, for the eighteenth century was prolific in its recording of contemporary affairs.[14] What alters the scenario appreciably was that a solid middle class was developing. England was becoming a nation of shop keepers, and many of them were prospering financially.[15] Despite the snobbery of the British upper class, they considered this growing middle class respectable and cautiously accepted some of them into their own ranks when fortunes had been amassed and land holdings were purchased.[16] This newly accepted middle class gave a boost of solidity and strength to the society, and its members became the producers of much of the creative thought of the industrial and agricultural revolutions.

The agricultural revolution in England was marked by a major land reform. Prior to the 1700's, England's farm land had been divided into small strips which were privately tilled by one family, with the returns commonly pooled by the commu-

---

[13]Frederick W. Hillis, ed., The Age of Johnson (New Haven: Yale University Press, 1949), p. 308.

[14]Gloag and Walter, Home Life in History, p. 234.

[15]Turberville, Men and Manners in the Eighteenth Century, p. 10.

[16]Asa Briggs, The Age of Improvement (London: Longmans, Green and Co., 1959), p. 11.

nity. It was realized that this was an enormous waste of man-power and effort. This "open-field" method of agriculture was then consolidated into large tracts of land, owned by one indi-vidual.[17] This change in agricultural land design (enclosures) reaped more benefits than just an amalgamation of labor. When the production from the land strips was controlled by a commu-nity of owners, there was little incentive for improvement. With enclosed large tracts of lands, each landowner was inde-pendent of his neighbor, free to introduce innovations in breeding and planting.[18]

Robert Bakewell experimented in animal husbandry, changing the ubiquitous English sheep from looking like an odd dog-like goat, to what we recognize today. Through his and others' ex-perimentation, the weight of stock animals increased appre-ciably. By the end of the 1700's, sheep and cattle weights had risen 2½ to 3 times.[19] With more meat on each animal, meat prices could remain reasonable. Experimentation was also going on in agriculture. Lord Townshend introduced the turnip, an easy to grow, easy to store, nutritious, cheap type of produce. Jethro Tull developed seed drilling and horse hoeing which im-proved production.[20] Other farming innovations made it pos-sible to grow wheat. Now rich and poor alike ate white bread,

---

[17]Snoden, A Mighty Ferment, p. 22.

[18]J. H. Plumb, England in the Eighteenth Century: 1714-1815 (Harmondsworth, Middlesex: Penguin Books, 1950), p. 82.

[19]Ibid., p. 83.

[20]Ibid., p. 18.

which the poor considered a phenomenal feat. The development
of new grass and root crops kept herds alive during the winter
months. Gone was the bleak winter diet of salted meats.[21]

Despite all the improvements the new enclosure system created, its one serious drawback was that it deprived the small
farmer of his land strip. They now had to become farm laborers
on the lands of the wealthy or go to the cities. These small
freeholders or yeomen, who numbered close to 180,000 strong in
the seventeenth century, had practically disappeared by the end
of the eighteenth.[22] The loss of a whole social class whose
members were conscientious and hard working was lamentable.
Oliver Goldsmith wrote:

> Ill fares the land, to hastening ills a prey,
> Where wealth accumulates, and men decay;
> Princes and lords may flourish, or may fade:
> But a bold peasantry, their country's pride
> When once destroyed, can never be supplied.[23]

Previously self sufficient, honest laborers were now often des-
titute, left to their parish for charity or to the new factories to work under horrendous conditions. The anguish and de-
plorable living conditions of this newly made lower class would
in the later part of the century move the consciences of the
upper classes to action.

As agriculture began to improve, and the whole of the
English countryside began to take on a new shape, there was

---

[21]Ibid., p. 83.

[22]Turberville, Men and Manners in the Eighteenth Century,
p. 136.

[23]Ibid., p. 141.

simultaneously a burst of interest and exploration into the
sciences. The discoveries that ensued marked the dawn of the
industrial revolution. Some historians feel that the industrial revolution has been enormously overrated. The majority of
the English up through the first half of the nineteenth century
were only indirectly affected.[24] However, the importance of
the industrial revolution lies not in the mechanization, but
rather in man's successful attempt "to master natural forces
which hitherto had mastered man."[25] The whole concept of the
biblical universe that the British had believed in with unques-
tioning faith, was now being shaken.[26] There was an awakening
to the fact that man had far more control and power over nature, and that nature itself had far more diversity than anyone
heretofore had believed.

The most significant mechanical discovery for the early
industrial revolution was the ability to harness steam to do
man's work. In 1769, James Watt (using concepts developed by
earlier inventors such as Savery and Newcomer)[27] invented the
steam engine. Never again would man be totally dependent upon
natural sources of power. The metal working and cloth indus-
tries were most affected at first from the new discoveries. In

---

[24]Muriel Jaeger, Before Victoria: Changing Standards and
Behaviors 1787-1837 (Harmondsworth, Middlesex: Penguin Books,
1956), p. 121.

[25]Briggs, The Age of Improvement, p. 18.

[26]Plumb, England in the Eighteenth Century, p. 28.

[27]Snoden, A Mighty Ferment, p. 25.

the first half of the century, Darby invented the process of using coke for smelting iron, "without this invention and its wide diffusion, England would not have led in the industrial revolution."[28] Major inventions for improving cloth production occurred in rapid succession. Hargreaves' Spinning Jenny could spin as many as 100 threads at a time. The water-frame invented by Arkwright utilized the power of water to operate the spinning machines. Crompton combined the Spinning Jenny with the water-frame to create a new apparatus which he appropriately named the "mule" to spin a finer textured yarn. Cartwright's Power Loom used water for the rapid weaving of cotton.[29] A new Britain was emerging, the product of this rapid technological change.[30] The old world with its pre-ordained structure was being subjected to sharp strains and stresses.[31]

Social beliefs and attitudes were further strained by the French Revolution. The notion of the fixed absolute "Scale" or "Order" seemed now out of place. Man, through his inventions and scientific inquiries had changed the shape and size of animals, created new varieties of plant life. If the natural world could be so drastically and dramatically altered, what of the economic stratification of social class? The French Revolution proved that within a few months, a monarchy established

---

[28]Plumb, England in the Eighteenth Century, p. 24.

[29]Turberville, Men and Manners in the Eighteenth Century, p. 77.

[30]Plumb, England in the Eighteenth Century, p. 77.

[31]Briggs, The Age of Improvement, p. 17.

for centuries could tumble. At first the fall of the Bastille
was greeted with applause by the liberal minded sections of
British society. They saw it as an imitation of their own revolution of 1688.[32] In the literary and artistic circles, the
first year of the revolution was immensely popular. It symbol-
ized the end of despotism in state and church and the chance
for individuals to achieve a new fulfillment, analogous to the
new achievements in Britain at the time.

However in 1793, when Louis XVI and Marie Antoinette were
executed and the revolution collapsed into the Reign of Terror,
public sentiment quickly changed. Edmund Burke wrote in his
Reflections on the Revolution that it was the destruction of
everything that was fine and valuable in society--learning,
grace, tolerance, order. When he continued to say that "a perfect democracy is the most shameless thing in the world," many
of England's upper classes nodded in agreement.[33] The French
revolution showed without any question the strength of the
middle and lower classes, and their ability if they so desired,
to achieve political leadership through revolutionary and vio-
lent means.[34] The British intellectuals who had at first wel-
comed the revolution suffered a serious disillusionment. Many
became reactionaries or morosely silent.[35] A conservatism that
had been developing from the early 1760's was reaching full

---

[32]Jaeger, Before Victoria, p. 45.

[33]Snoden, A Mighty Ferment, p. 42.

[34]Plumb, England in the Eighteenth Century, p. 155.

[35]Snoden, A Mighty Ferment, p. 43.

force in the 1790's. The upper-middle classes and aristocracy
wanted no change in institutions, and all groups that carried a
banner or slogan were labeled "enthusiasts" or revolutionaries.[36]

The eighteenth century opened and closed with "enthusiasts" being suspect. The century began ultra conservative in
attitude and ended ultra conservative in attitude. But this
was in no means a mere duplication of social thought and manner. Far too many changes had occurred. The conservatism at
the end of the century was characterized by humanitarian concerns, religious revivals, and sentimentalism. This was not
seen earlier. It was also affected by the enormous gain in
scientific knowledge which promoted a growing belief in the
enormous capabilities of the human spirit.

It should be clearly pointed out that the conservatism
which permeated English society in the latter half of the century was not opposed to certain forms of social change. Although there was a strong desire to prevent sweeping structural
changes, England was developing a conscience.[37] This sense of
duty, of conscience, however led to both reform and repression.
On the positive side, social reformers far too numerous to mention by name, filled the country's periodicals and literature
with pleas to help all men socially and spiritually.[38] Socie-
ties of all sorts and of varying degrees of political strength

---

[36] Jaeger, Before Victoria, p. 45.

[37] Hillis, The Age of Johnson, p. 315.

[38] D. M. Yarde, The Life and Works of Sarah Trimmer (The
Hounslow District Historical Society, 1972), p. 2.

sprang up in rapid succession to improve the lot of men. One

typical example was the Society of Bettering the Condition of

the Poor. The intention of the Society according to their

first public report was "the inquiry into all that concerns the

poor and promotion of their happiness [to be developed into] a

science."[39] Sunday Schools were established to help the chil-

dren of the poor be profitably employed on the Sabbath. Read-

ing, writing, and basic arithmetic were taught. Industry

schools were formed to teach the poor, new trades and use of

the new equipment. A whole new body of literature was devised

to give the lower classes proper reading materials. Charity

hospitals and foundling homes began to appear in significant

numbers.

These social reforms were created not to raise the poor

from their station in life, but rather to make them generally

happier, more productive as workers, and help them become bet-

ter Christians. Only a few forward thinking individuals could

see the obvious repercussions of these reforms, especially the

educational ones. One such individual wrote at the time, "Hard

toil and humble diligence are indispensably needful to the com-

munity . . . . Writing and accounts appear supercilious in-

structions in the humblest walks of life; and when imparted to

servants, have the general effect of making them ambitious and

disgusted with the servile offices which they are required to

_____

[39]Briggs, The Age of Improvement, p. 16.

perform."[40] This writer was correct in her assessment. The
social reforms affected the lower classes far more than they
were intended to. Also, they were extremely important for pav-
ing the way for larger structural changes such as the establishment of public education. Unquestionably for the poorer
citizens of the late eighteenth century, these reforms offered
opportunities and services that had not been available before--
hospital care, a large network of charitable organizations and
education. This certainly bettered their lot and perhaps
helped to prevent a revolution. There was another repercussion
of these social reforms. They made the upper-middle and upper
classes enormously pleased with themselves. As Sir John Haw-
kins wrote in 1787, "We live in an age when humanity is in
fashion."[41] There was good reason for this self satisfaction.
They were able to bring about important social reform, without
destroying the basic tenets of their social structure. The
late eighteenth century was a period filled with conservative
do-gooders.

Evolving side by side with this conservative reform was a
back-to-basics ideology in religion. Although in the case of
John Wesley, this led to an actual cleavage from the Church of
England, for the most part, the religious revival led to atti-
tudinal changes within the Anglican Church. Wilberforce (best
known today for his work for the abolition of slavery) was a

---

[40]Agnes Repplier, A Happy Half Century and Other Essays
(Boston: Houghton Mifflin, 1908), p. 186.

[41]Briggs, The Age of Improvement, p. 13.

forceful proponent for religious reform. He pushed in Parliament for the passing of the Royal Proclamation of 1787 against Vice and Immorality.[42] This was a law prohibiting Sabbath breaking, swearing, licentious publications, and other lewd behaviors. There had always been laws against such actions, but no one seriously considered enforcing them. What marked this proclamation apart from other laws was the strict observation of the Sabbath. Rationally, the other sections of the laws were defensible. Heavy gambling, excessive drinking, sexual promiscuity, are not usually considered desirable for a society--morally, economically or medically. This kind of reasoning cannot be applied to strict Sabbath observance; laws that are commanded in the Bible. This proclamation defied a social climate structured by rationality and reason.[43]

The new revival in the Anglican church has been called by some a "New Puritanism."[44] Frivolity was now frowned upon, an austerity of personal decorum and self introspection became fashionable. Theater, amusing conversation, and light pleasure reading were looked upon by the more fanatical as ungodly and a sure path to Hell. This attitude was a marked contrast to the liberal and licentious life styles followed by the upper classes earlier in the century. The efforts of early eighteenth century theologians to reconcile religion with reason

---

[42]Jaeger, _Before Victoria_, p. 24.

[43]_Ibid._, p. 26.

[44]_Ibid._, p. 43.

were now frowned upon. The Puritan's fiery brimstone was re-
kindled, guilt and wrongdoing now received intense personal introspection. Everlasting salvation was sought. One repercussion of this was a reactionary conservatism, with its hostility
to innovation.[45] Another was a dulling of the joie de vivre.
Hannah More wrote, "The Amusements of a Christian must have
nothing in them to excite the passions which it is his duty to
subdue; they must not obstruct spiritual-mindedness, nor en-
flame the lust of the flesh, lust of the eye and pride of
life."[46]

The social changes in both attitude and behavior of the
eighteenth century were caused by many factors. The growth of
scientific inquiry led to enormous strides in agricultural and
industrial production. This created prosperity and gave a
greater sense of confidence in the abilities in man. In turn,
this faith in mankind led to a burst of philanthropic activities. Yet with the changes that the agricultural and industrial revolutions brought, it is understandable that a spiritu-
al confusion could occur. The countryside had literally been
transformed, man was able to create things that before were
left to the realm of Divine Providence. The rationality that
was in part caused by this growth of scientific exploration
left a void, which the religious revivals filled. The renewed
interest in religion furthered the growth of charitable work,

---

[45]Repplier, A Happy Half Century and Other Essays, p. 186.

[46]Jaeger, Before Victoria, p. 28.

for beneficence and concern for helping others falls under the definition of Christian love.[47] With the religious revivals came a conservatism, at times reactionary. The new literal interpreting of the Bible was a far cry from the liberal, open-minded attitudes of the first part of the century. This growing conservatism was given further fuel by the anarchy that resulted from the French revolution.

This was the time in which the didactic children's writers emerged. These authors were not part of the avant garde, they were not bohemians. They were individuals who reflected the trends and complexities of their age. Their lives in many respects were quite typical of the upper middle classes. The major differences were perhaps the internal ones of intelligence, motivation, and energy.

Attitudes Toward Women

To understand and properly interpret literary works, one must be aware of the social and historical events that helped to mold the writers' thinking. It is also important to be aware of the significant events in the lives of the writers and understand how the contemporary society viewed the authors themselves. This should go beyond the acclaim or criticism they received, one must understand the attitudes toward their profession, and in this case, to their sex. The writers chosen

---

[47]Brian W. Downs, Richardson (London: George Routledge, 1928), p. 170.

for this investigation are all women. This choice was not done as a feminist statement, but rather because it was these authors, who happen to be women, who best (in this writer's mind, at least) characterize the first true writing for children: Writing specifically created not for financial gain, not to propagandize a specific religious or philosophical belief, but for the child's enjoyment and moral development.

Women of the eighteenth century were viewed far differently than in our present century. These societal attitudes toward the gentle sex were caused by a complex interaction of forces. As shown in the preceding section, the industrial and agricultural revolutions, the French revolution and the religious revival movement dramatically changed attitudes and mores in the second half of the eighteenth century. Of all of these, the religious revival was perhaps the most important in both influencing attitudes toward women and in turn influencing the women themselves. With the passing in Parliament of Wilberforce's Proclamation of 1787 and the rise of Wesleyanism, the Bible was reexamined, its tenets believed literally. St. Paul's definition of the role of women was studied and adhered to by many. He wrote:

> In like manner also the women adorn themselves in
> modest apparel, with shamefacedness and sobri-
> ety, not with broided hair, or gold or pearls
> or costly array.
> But (which becometh women professing godliness)
> with good works.
> Let the women learn in silence and with all
> subjection.[48]

---

[48]Jaeger, Before Victoria, pp. 117-118.

This view especially regarding dress was quite different from the fashion codes of the first half of the century when it reached the state of the ridiculous with foot high hairpieces and tottering high-heeled shoes. No doubt a change in fashion was needed, if not for aesthetic reasons, at least for comfort. This modesty was not just followed for the external appearance, the internal "shamefacedness" was also unquestionably adopted by many as the proper mode for feminine behavior. Women also followed St. Paul's words about adorning themselves with good works. Hannah More, in her Strictures on the Modern System of Female Education wrote that every young woman should become an amateur social worker.[49] To do good, to better the lot of others, to train the young in the proper morals were the few avenues open to the middle and upper class women who sought a life outside of being a wife and mother. Writing for the young, especially in the didactic mode, fulfilled these requirements.

Writing in general, during the second half of the eighteenth century, became more and more acceptable--lady writers increased in epidemic proportions. Not only did it seem that every woman of distinguished rank took pen in hand, but they also enjoyed a degree of fame and fortune that was at times, utterly disproportionate to their merits.[50] But these women

[49]Maurice J. Quinlin, Victorian Prelude: A History of English Manners 1700-1830 (Hamden, Conn.: Archon Books, 1965), p. 155.

[50]Repplier, A Happy Half Century and Other Essays, pp. 2-3.

writers had to create within the narrowly defined social param-
eters. In keeping with the concept of modesty, it was common
for them to write anonymously.[51] Their writing could not demonstrate any form of passion, for that emotion was incompatible
with the inner delicacy of the female being.[52] To be accepted,
a woman writer also had to be known as a person of virtue.
Mrs. Montague wrote to the then unwed Mrs. Barbauld, Anna
Aiken, after her first publication, "I made many inquiries into
your character . . . ," and happily found her moral character
was as elevated as her mental accomplishments.[53]

This preponderance of feminine writers is not surprising
since it was one of the few ways in which they could express
themselves artistically and intellectually in public. In the
1750's Mrs. Montague wrote in regard to her granddaughter's
education, "conceal whatever learning she attains with as much
solicitude as she would hide crookedness or lameness."[54] This
attitude of feigned feminine stupidity prevailed through the
eighteenth and well into the nineteenth century. Eventually
the concealment of learning turned into no learning at all.
Education for young ladies became less formal and more

---

[51]Jaeger, _Before Victoria_, p. 34.

[52]P. H. Newby, _Maria Edgeworth_ (Denver: Allan Swallow,
1950), p. 6.

[53]Catherine J. Hamilton, _Women Writers: Their Works and
Ways_, 1st series (Freeport, N.Y.: Books for Libraries Press,
1971, originally published, 1882), p. 70.

[54]Christina Hole, _English Home Life: 1500-1800_ (London:
B. T. Batsford Ltd., 1947), p. 124.

frivolous as the nineteenth century neared. In the 1750's, girls were expected to have a proficiency in English, French, and penmanship. The reading of classics and even the study of Latin was not unheard of. By the end of the century, the upper classes were schooled in mediocrity. They were taught the "ornamental arts." They learned to make "filigree baskets that would not hold anything . . . taking impressions of butterflies' wings on sheets of gummed paper, and messing with strange, mysterious compounds called diaphanie and potichomanie, by means of which a harmless glass tumbler or a respectable window pane could be turned into an object of desolation."[55]

The reasoning behind this frivolity was that a woman should not be highly trained and should "learn in silence and with all subjection." As Mrs. Trimmer wrote about the educating of young girls, "Drawing might be safely acquired, provided only that care be taken not to excite vanity."[56] There seems to be an implicit message here that excellence should not be stressed, for it may lead to self pride and the loss of modesty. Reading matter for girls and women was also censored. Strong admonitions were given to parents against allowing their daughters to borrow from circulating libraries. Books such as Tom Jones were naturally forbidden, but far tamer pieces of fiction were looked at suspiciously.[57]

---

[55] Repplier, A Happy Half Century and Other Essays, pp. 217-218.

[56] Yarde, The Life and Works of Sarah Trimmer, p. 44.

[57] Quinlin, Victorian Prelude, p. 145.

Women in the late eighteenth century were expected to be modest, chaste in dress and action, display no overt signs of intelligence (except in written form), be servile in attitude, and perform charitable works. This was the setting in which the Kilners, Mrs. Barbauld, Mrs. Trimmer, and Miss Edgeworth were writing. Fortunately, most of their early education was not influenced by the "ornamental art" theory of pedagogy. Yet their general outlook on life, unquestionably reflected the subservient role of women, the need for modesty, and the accepted goals for women in society. Mrs. Trimmer became one of the leaders in establishing Sunday Schools for the poor. Her modesty was never questioned, and her attitude in public was marked by "refined diffidence."[58] Maria Edgeworth remained always the dutiful daughter and learned "in silence and with all subjection" from her father. Mrs. Barbauld gave her life to good works and education. She was devoted to her mentally ill husband, only leaving him when her life was in danger. As seen by her contemporaries, such "suffering [had] been in a noble cause."[59] The Kilners were so "shamefaced" that they published anonymously and had very little to do with publicity. Yet these women were enormously bright and talented. In keeping with societal dictates, they used their talents in one of the few acceptable avenues for female thought, writing. Their

---

[58]Repplier, A Happy Half Century and Other Essays, p. 119.

[59]Mrs. Ellis, The Wives of England: Their Relative Duties, Domestic Influence, and Social Obligations (New York: D. Appleton, 1843), p. 104.

writing was deemed even more proper because it dealt with
teaching the young morality. If they had lived in a later age,
one wonders how they would have used their talents. Luckily
for the children they were not and left a legacy of charming
and innovative writings.

A Biographical Sketch of Mary Jane (Ann?) Kilner and Dorothy Kilner

In a small village of only thirty-four houses, called
Maryland Point (now incorporated into London, but then in a re-
mote part of Essex),[60] lived two literary ladies by the name of
Kilner. The town no longer exists. Its memory is kept only by
a small railroad station in the northeast section of London.
The memory of the ladies, like the town, ostensibly seems except for brief references here or there to have disappeared.
In keeping with the contemporary view of feminine modesty,
these ladies wished for no public acclaim or notice. Their
children's books were published under various pseudonyms or
with no name at all. Much to the frustration of this researcher, they were extremely successful in their desire for anonym-
ity.[61] In comparison to Mrs. Trimmer, Mrs. Barbauld, and Maria

[60]Mary Ann Kilner, Memoirs of a Peg-Top (London: Marshall, 178?, reprint ed., New York: Garland, 1977), p. vi.

[61]Modest as they were, the Kilners were not beyond advertising their books within another. In Dorothy Kilner's school
stories, the prize awarded to the best scholar was another
Kilner book. Gillespie finds fault with "puffing their wares"
in this manner. Margaret Gillespie, Literature for Children--
History and Trends (Dubuque, Iowa: William C. Brown, 1970), p.
86. What the Kilners did, was not at all uncommon and was an
advertising ploy often used by John Newbery.

Edgeworth, of whom much has been written, the information on the Kilners is scarce and that which is found is contradictory.

Dorothy Kilner (1755-1836) is perhaps today the best known of the two. Working under the pseudonym of M. P. (probably after the village of her residence), she later adopted the writing name of Mary Pelham at the suggestion of her publisher.[62] Mary Jane Kilner (1753-?) is more of an enigma. Even her Christian name is disputed. Most of the texts and commentators refer to her as Mary Jane, although antiquarian book sellers cite her as Mary Ann. Her kinship to Dorothy is also in doubt. Darton, Patterson, Meigs and others, refer to the women as sisters, while Thwaite and Osbourne have defined their relationship as sisters-in-law, using as Mary Jane's maiden name, Maze. Despite the lack of information on them today, they were well respected and popular authors in their day. Their publisher, John Marshall, delightedly advertised their books as being "a different style from the Generality of Works designed for young People."[63] Justin Schiller, a prominent New York City antiquarian book seller, feels that Dorothy Kilner's Life and Perambulations of a Mouse (1783) was as popular as Goody Two Shoes in the eighteenth century.[64] The

---

[62]Judith St. John, ed., The Osbourne Collection of Early Children's Books: 1566-1910 (Toronto: Toronto Public Library, 1958), p. 273.

[63]Cornelia Meigs, Elizabeth Nesbill, Anne T. Eaton, and Ruth Viguers, A Critical History of Children's Literature (New York: Macmillan, 1967), p. 92.

[64]Discussed in a phone conversation, Philadelphia to New York, April 1982.

Kilners were invited to contribute to one of the earliest periodicals for children, The Juvenile Magazine. Although it ran
for only one year, 1788, it was very fashionable with sheet
music, folding maps, and stories by well known authors.[65] The
Kilners' books were popular enough to be published in America
by Isaiah Thomas.[66] Some of their stories were taken out of
their original context and reprinted by American printing
houses in a series of four didactic books.[67] Although this
series was designed to provide "the young reader with a few
pages which should be innocent of corrupting if they did not
amuse,"[68] one hopes the young readers were entertained by them.

Dorothy Kilner published at least ten books ranging from a
sprightly story of four mice and their adventures to religious
treatises such as The First Principles of Religion, Dialogues
on Morality, A Clear . . . Account of the Origins and Design of
Christianity. One of her more popular books was The Village
School, intended to censor the vices of boarding schools.[69]
The main characters were Jacob Steadfast and Ralph Breakclop--

---

[65]Eric Quale, The Collector's Book of Children's Books
(New York: Clarkson N. Potter, 1971), p. 117.

[66]Sylvia W. Patterson, Rousseau's Emile and Early Children's Literature (Metuchen, New Jersey: Scarecrow Press,
1971), p. 133.

[67]Rosalie Halsey, Forgotten Books of the American Nursery:
A History of the Development of the American Story-Book (Boston: Charles E. Goodspeed, 1911), p. 111.

[68]Ibid., p. 112.

[69]F. J. Harvey Darton, Children's Books in England: Five
Centuries of Social Life (Cambridge: Cambridge University,
1958), p. 165.

need one have to point out which is the good boy and which the
bad? Undoubtedly, her best work was The Life and Perambulations of a Mouse. It has been suggested that this work had
been influenced by Mrs. Trimmer's Fabulous Histories.[70] There
is evidence that the women were friends, and that Miss Kilner
sent manuscripts to Mrs. Trimmer to critique.[71] Dorothy Kilner's volume, however, was first published in 1783(?), Fabulous
Histories came out in 1786. Unless she had heard the story
from Mrs. Trimmer, which is possible since Mrs. Trimmer had
written the story earlier for the amusement of her own children, one has to question the influence of Fabulous Histories
on Miss Kilner's mouse tale. There is evidence, however, that
Mrs. Trimmer was extremely pleased with the book and in her
Guardian of Education she described it as "one of the prettiest
and most instructive books that can be found for young readers.
A book, indeed which Mothers and even Grandmothers may read
with interest and pleasure."[72] Dorothy Kilner, like Mrs. Trimmer, Mrs. Barbauld, and Maria Edgeworth originally began writing, not for publication purposes but to amuse her young
relatives.[73]

---

[70]Meigs, et al., A Critical History of Children's Literature, p. 92.

[71]Mrs. Field, A Child and His Book (London: Wells Gardner, Darton and Co., 1892), p. 268.

[72]Mrs. Trimmer, The Guardian of Education, Vol. I (London:
J. Hatchard, 1802), pp. 435-436.

[73]St. John, ed., The Osbourne Collection of Early Books,
p. 273.

Mary Jane (Ann?) Kilner started her children's writing on a somber note with A Course of Lectures for Sunday Evenings, containing Religious Advice for Young Persons.[74] How little children reading the book responded one does not know; but in the story the eldest daughter, listening to her father's reading of "serious truths," tilted her head to the side, with eyelids heavy, "fell into a profound sleep, interrupted only by involuntary starts when in danger of falling."[75] The dreariness of her father's sermons can probably not be disputed, but what is pertinent is Mrs. Kilner's awareness of the nature of children and what bores them. Her innovative stories, The Adventures of a Pincushion, written for the feminine gender, and its masculine counterpart, The Memoirs of a Peg Top, did not put their young readers asleep. These stories are told by the afore-named inanimate objects. She apologizes for this flight of fancy (which in the late eighteenth century was not considered appropriate for the young) by writing, "it is to be understood as an imaginary tale in the same manner as when you are at play, you sometimes call yourselves gentlemen and ladies, though you know you are only little boys and girls."[76] Once again, her compassion and understanding of the young is demonstrated.

Mrs. Jill Grey is currently writing a book on the Kilners,

---

[74]Darton, Children's Books in England, p. 165.

[75]Ibid., p. 166.

[76]Meigs, et al., A Critical History of Children's Literature, p. 93.

and this hopefully will clarify the existing confusion about these women as well as giving them greater recognition.

A Biographical Sketch of Maria Edgeworth

Maria Edgeworth was born in 1767. Her father Richard Lovell Edgeworth was a dynamic, brilliant, and somewhat eccentric man. Her mother, Anna Maria, died a few years after her birth. Maria however was not to be motherless for long. Richard in all took four wives, and fathered twenty-one children. As the second child and eldest daughter, Maria had enormous responsibilities, which she obviously took over gladly. Despite the succession of mothers and frequent arrival of younger siblings, the Edgeworth home was a seemingly happy one. Richard Edgeworth reported, "I do not think one tear per month is shed in the house, nor the voice of reproof heard, nor the hand of restraint felt."[77] The only one not so contented was the eldest son, Richard, who was strictly educated according to Rousseau's philosophy, with Thomas Day monitoring the situation. This experiment was a disaster. Young Richard was incorrigible, and eventually was shipped off to sea.[78]

Maria fortunately escaped her brother's fate. Richard Edgeworth senior, a man deeply concerned with educational theory, used far more temperance and common sense in the education

---

[77]Mrs. Florence Barry, A Century of Children's Books (London: Methuen and Co., 1922), p. 176.

[78]Grace A. Oliver, A Study of Maria Edgeworth (Boston: A. Williams and Co., 1882), pp. 51-52.

of his eldest daughter. In antithesis to the prevailing notions of schooling for young ladies at the time, he believed
that only a liberal education could guide the development and
growth of the female character, enabling her to best adjust to
society and achieve happiness in general.[79] In keeping with
this theory, Maria was not sheltered from family business.
When the Edgeworths moved to the family estate, Edgeworthstown
in Ireland, she actively participated with her father in fulfilling the landlord's duty: collecting the rent, solving
neighborhood disputes, and copying his letters of business.[80]
This gave her an intimate knowledge of the Irish peasant whom
she so vividly portrayed in her adult novels.

Her formal writing career began modestly in 1782 with her
father's suggestion to translate from the French, Adele et
Theodore, an extremely popular children's story by Madame de
Genles. Mr. Edgeworth originally proposed this project to provide his daughter with a profitable activity to occupy her leisure hours. He later changed his orientation (perhaps due to
the quality of the manuscript) and began thinking in terms of
publication. This plan was never carried through because a
translation of the same book, by a Mr. Holcroft, was printed
before Maria had finished hers.[81] This, however, was not her

---

[79]Elva S. Smith, The History of Children's Literature, revised by Margaret Hodges and Susan Steinfast (Chicago: American Library Association, 1980), p. 112.

[80]Newby, Maria Edgeworth, pp. 22-23.

[81]When Thomas Day heard about the plans he was horrified
at the thought that a woman was attempting such a work. When

first attempt at writing. To amuse the ever expanding Edgeworth brood, Maria wrote "wee, wee stories" to amuse and in-
struct her brothers and sisters. Usually these tales were
written on a slate; only after they won the approval of the
household and suitable corrections were made, did they get
copied out in ink.[82] Probably no author, past or present, has
had such an excellent opportunity to consistently judge the reaction of the prospective juvenile audience.[83]

The approval of this ready made audience was undoubtedly
important and helped motivate Miss Edgeworth to write, but unquestionably the most important influence in her life was her
father. Theirs was a close, loving, yet patriarchal relationship. Of his influence, Maria wrote, "Whenever I thought of
writing anything, I always told him my first rough plans; and
always, with the instinct of a good critic, he used to fix immediately upon that which would best answer the purpose.
'Sketch that, and shew it to me.' These words, from the experience of his sagacity, never failed to inspire me with a hope
of success."[84] Many modern critics are under the impression

---

publication was impossible, Mr. Day congratulated his lifelong
friend on not having to be embarrassed by a daughter who was a
translating author. Hamilton, Women Writers, p. 163.

[82]Maria Edgeworth, Castle Rackrent and the Absentee, introduction by Brandes Matthew (London: J. M. Dent, n.d.), p.
ix.

[83]Annie E. Moore, Literature Old and New for Children
(Cambridge, Mass.: Houghton Mifflin, 1934), p. 194.

[84]Dobson, Austin, "The Parent's Assistant," Delibris:
Prose and Verse (London: Macmillan, 1911), Lance Salway, ed.,
reprint Signal 17 (May 1975): 100.

that her father's overwhelming influence hurt Maria's style,
squelching the spontaneity and narrative flow. Richard Edgeworth states himself how unmerciful his criticism was. In 1805
he wrote after reading one of his daughter's drafts, "cut out a
few pages, one or two letters are nearly untouched, the rest
are cut, scrawled, and underlined without mercy."[85] In analyzing Richard Edgeworth's influence, Catherine Hamilton in 1892
wrote,

> Some say now that Maria Edgeworth would have done
> much better if she had been left to herself,
> without her father's perpetual criticism, but
> this seems more than doubtful. She had little
> confidence in herself, and he gave her confi-
> dence; and she wanted someone on whom her judg-
> ment could rely, and he supplied this want. She
> wrote on freely, knowing that he would find out
> anything that was incorrect and superfluous, and
> so confidence came. Without it a writer is on
> crutches.[86]

Maria's own words support this hypothesis. After her father's
death she wrote,

> He inspired in my mind a degree of hope and con-
> fidence essential in the first instance to the
> full exertion of the mental powers, and necessary
> to ensure perseverance in any occupation. Such,
> happily for me, was his power over my mind that
> no one thing I ever begun to write was ever left
> unfinished.[87]

Once Maria began to write formally, the publications came
out in rapid succession. In 1795, she published <u>Letters for
Literary Ladies</u> which strongly reflected her father's views on

---

[85]Meigs, et al., <u>Critical History of Children's Litera-
ture</u>, p. 102.

[86]Hamilton, <u>Women Writers</u>, p. 164.

[87]Newby, <u>Maria Edgeworth</u>, p. 17.

educating young women. Although the views professed were tepid
in comparison to Mary Wollstonecraft's Vindication of the
Rights of Women (1792), it did encourage a solid education for
girls, for "her mind must be enlarged . . . her knowledge must
be various and her powers of reasoning unawed by authority."[88]
Maria, however, did not follow her own advice, since her reasoning was surely awed by her father's dictates. In contrast
to Miss Wollstonecraft's treatise, Maria Edgeworth's book was
widely accepted and gained an immediate reputation for its
author. This is because Letters for Literary Ladies never suggested any radical departure from the prescribed notions of
feminine behavior. "The imagination of the young lady," wrote
Miss Edgeworth, "must never be raised above the taste for necessary occupations, or the numerous small but trifling pleasures of domestic life . . . the delicacy of her manners must be
preserved."[89] In 1798, she co-authored with her father, Practical Education. Based upon a twenty-two year old anecdotal
record of the Edgeworth children's comments, activities, and
behaviors,[90] this treatise was a pioneer work in child study.
Its basic premise was that learning is an active process, which
was an extremely modern thought for its day.[91] It was a

---

[88]Quinlin, Victorian Prelude, p. 143.

[89]Newby, Maria Edgeworth, p. 30.

[90]Hamilton, Women Writers, p. 163.

[91]Anonymous, "Edgeworth Family: Anticipators of Froebel,"
New York Times 1778, education supplement (May 27, 1949):
335.

popular and well respected book[92] and was still so widely used
in 1848 that William Chamber, a successful publisher, decided
to pick it up for reprinting.[93]

The Parent's Assistant was written as a companion to Practical Education. The purpose of these stories, wrote Richard
Edgeworth in the preface, was "to provide antidotes against ill
humour . . . to avoid inflaming the imagination . . . or exciting a useless spirit of adventure." Also it was written to improve the moralistic school of writing of the day. He hoped
these stories would "prevent the precepts of morality from tiring the ear and mind" by including some dramatic elements "to
keep alive hope, fear and curiosity by some degree of intricacy."[94] These stories were immediately successful. A second
printing ensued in 1797, and in 1800 it was reissued as an expanded six-volume set.[95] The only disappointment Maria had
about these stories was its title, "My father had sent [the

[92]Mrs. Trimmer wrote about this treatise, "We have already
borne testimony to this work as a very ingenious composition,
and we are ready to allow that abounds with practical observations, from which those who are engaged in the instruction of
children may collect many valuable hints for the management of
their tempers and the cultivation of their intellectual facul-
ties." However she could not give it a wholehearted approval,
since it did not include any religious teaching. Trimmer,
Guardian of Education, Vol. I, p. 490.

[93]Anonymous, "Edgeworth Family: Anticipators of Froebel,"
p. 335.

[94]Maria Edgeworth, The Parent's Assistant, Vol. I, introduction by Richard Lovell Edgeworth (London: Baldwin, Cradock,
and Joy, 1822), p. x.

[95]Dobson, "The Parent's Assistant," Salway, ed., Signal,
May 1975, p. 98.

title] 'Parent's Friend,' but Mr. Johnson [the publisher] has degraded it in the 'Parent's Assistant,' which I dislike particularly, from association with an old book of arithmetic called the 'Tutor's Assistant.'"[96] In 1800, her Moral Tales were published, and soon after, Early Lessons and Popular Tales came into print. Under the careful scrutiny of Mrs. Trimmer, praise of Early Lessons and other Edgeworth books was given sparingly in The Guardian of Education; however, the general public seemed to clamor for more. Rosamond, a character first introduced in Parent's Assistant, was so popular that a whole series of stories about her were created.[97] Many of her other tales, like "Simple Susan," "Lazy Lawrence," "Harry and Lucy," and "The Bracelots" were republished in volumes by themselves due to popular demand.

Maria Edgeworth's literary fame was also due to her adult novels. In 1800, she published Castle Rackrent. Here, she introduced for the first time in literary history, an honest portrayal of the Irish peasant. Based on her earlier experiences with the peasants on her father's estate, she was able to write about the working classes with insight and compassion. This ability to develop characters and to vividly portray the Irish landscape brought her a prominence in her day equal to her contemporary Jane Austen.[98] In one sense, her adult

[96]M. Pollard, "Maria Edgeworth's The Parent's Assistant, The First Edition," Book Collector 20 (Autumn, 1971): 349.

[97]Meigs, et al., A Critical History of Children's Literature, p. 102.

[98]Edgeworth, Castle Rackrent, p. vi.

writing was superior to her books for children because in the
former she was able to develop the moral as a natural outgrowth
of the plot, rather than superimposing the moral upon the story
structure as she did more often in her juvenile writing.[99] Her
prominence as an author is also shown through her influence
upon other writers. Sir Walter Scott wrote that it was her interpretation and observation of Irish life that led him to move
away from Romantic poetry to writing novels about Scotland, its
people and countryside.[100] The great Russian novelist, Tur-
genev, author of Memoirs of a Sportsman (which some believe
sparked the abolition of serfdom), confessed that it was Miss
Edgeworth's sensitivity to the Irish peasant which showed him
the possibilities of representing the Russian working class in
a similar manner. J. F. Cooper and Thackeray also acknowledged
her influence. Characters and episodes created by both of
these men were based upon Maria's writing.[101]

　　Although Maria Edgeworth was extremely respected and admired in her profession, this did not preclude her following
the established rules of feminine etiquette and decorum. As
shown before, writing was an acceptable activity for women in
the eighteenth century. She was very much a woman of her day--
modest, humble, and respectful. One Saturday night in 1796,
she wrote meekly to a friend, "I beg, dear Sophy, that you will

---

[99]Ibid., p. xiii.

[100]Meigs, et al., A Critical History of Children's Literature, p. 103.

[101]Edgeworth, Castle Rackrent, p. xvi.

not call my little stories by the sublime title of 'my works.'
I shall else be ashamed when the little mouse comes forth."[102]
Thomas Moore said of her in 1818, "Miss Edgeworth [is] delightful, not from display, but from repose and unaffectedness, the
least pretending person of the company."[103] She remained always the devoted daughter, subservient and obedient. As her
father lay dying, she sank to her knees and promised "to be
good." She was fifty years old at the time.[104]

Her first duty was to her home and family. This sense of
duty and enormous sense of attachment, perhaps was the motivation behind her refusing the marriage proposal of a Monsieur
Edelcrantz, a Swedish gentleman of "mild manner and superior
understanding." She wrote of the proposal to a friend, "I
think nothing could ever tempt me to leave my own dear friends
and country to live in Sweden."[105] She was sensitive to others
and beneficent in thought and action. A contemporary wrote,
"Maria's tears are always ready when any generous string is
touched."[106]

Whether the gentle and modest Miss Edgeworth wished it or
not, she became a public figure. Despite her tiny size, and
what biographers and Maria herself considered a plain face, she

_____

[102]M. Pollard, "Maria Edgeworth's The Parent's Assistant,
The First Edition," Book Collector, Autumn, 1971, pp. 348-349.

[103]Hamilton, Women Writers, p. 172.

[104]Newby, Maria Edgeworth, p. 38.

[105]Hamilton, Women Writers, p. 169.

[106]Ibid., p. 168.

dominated polite society in the late eighteenth and early nineteenth century. Mrs. Barbauld reported that Maria Edgeworth was one of the most sought after people in London society. Sir Walter Scott received a letter from an author friend saying, "You would have been amused if you had seen with what eagerness people crowded to get sight of Miss Edgeworth . . . peeping over shoulders and between curled tetes to get but one look."[107]

At 83, Maria Edgeworth died on May 22, 1849 at her beloved Edgeworthstown. Her life was long and distinguished. She was undoubtedly the most gifted of the didactic group. It has only been in the last fifty years or so that her books, both adult novels and children's stories, have faded in popularity. Her children's stories are so intrinsically good, one wonders, if they were rewritten in more modern language if they would not once again catch the enthusiasm of the young?

A Biographical Sketch of Mrs. Anna Laetitia Aiken Barbauld

In the village of Kibworth Howard in Leicestershire, Anna Laetitia Aiken was born on June 20, 1743. She was exceedingly bright and by the age of two her mother wrote, she "could read sentences and little stories, in her wise book, roundly without spelling, and in half a year more could read as well as most women."[108] Soon after, she learned French and Italian, and

---

[107] Isabel C. Clarke, Maria Edgeworth: Her Family and Friends (London: Hutchinson and Co., n.d.), p. 90.

[108] Betsey Rodgers, Georgian Chronicles: Mrs. Barbauld and Her Family (London: Methuen and Co., 1958), p. 29.

with her father's reluctant permission, was studying Latin and Greek, at the age of six.[109] Anna Laetitia grew up in academic surroundings. Her father John, a Unitarian minister, taught at various boys' schools. This drew concern from her mother who worried that such environments would make her only daughter rough and ill-mannered. To counteract these influences, her mother raised her with the utmost decorum and propriety, making the mother-daughter relationship reserved and diffident, with neither of them being particularly cordial.[110] Because of her very proper early training, Anna felt herself unduly reserved and complained to a friend "of her awkwardness about common things."[111]

Despite her stern upbringing and critical view of herself, Anna Aiken Barbauld was known throughout her life for her wit, charm, and beauty. She may have seen herself as a cold, distant type of person, but through letters her wide circle of friends left a much different picture. One such letter described a marvelous dinner party that she hosted for some of the young men attending her father's school. Tempting morsels were placed before them, yet when the gentlemen proceeded to help themselves, they found the hams were made of wood, the potted beef created from sawdust, the trifles executed from soap suds. One long time admirer described her as possessing "great beauty,

---

[109] Field, The Child and His Book, p. 263.

[110] Rodgers, Georgian Chronicles, p. 30.

[111] Hamilton, Women Writers, p. 68.

distinct traces of which she retained to the latest of her life. Her person was slender, her complexion exquisitely fair with the bloom of perfect health, her features regular and elegant, and her dark blue eyes beamed with the light of wit and fancy." With such a description, it is not surprising that Miss Aiken had many suitors. One admirer was so persistent, that she had to escape from his advances by climbing a tree and then leaping over the garden wall.[112]

She spent most of her young adult life at Warrington and seemed most happy there. She enjoyed an extremely close relationship with her younger brother, John. She was also surrounded by a gay society of young people as well as a group of distinguished and learned men. It was at Warrington that she did her first formal writing. In 1773, she published her first volume of adult poems which received instant acclaim. Congratulations poured in, with special notes of praise from Dr. Priestly and Mrs. Montague.[113] The next year she was wed to Rochemont Barbauld. Their union was a surprising one, for it was well known that the Reverend Barbauld had a "strong taint of insanity, of which Anna was warned."[114] Some of Mrs. Barbauld's biographers wrote of the marriage with concern. Misses Elwood and Hamilton, two nineteenth century writers, felt that she did not regret her choice as much as her friends did. Even

---

[112] Rodgers, Georgian Chronicles, pp. 51-52.

[113] Hamilton, Women Writers, pp. 69-70.

[114] Ibid., p. 73.

in Mr. Barbauld's deepest moments of despair, "the kindness of his nature broke forth, and some of his last acts were acts of benevolence."[115]

The couple began their married life teaching at a boys' school in Palgrave. This was a happy and productive time for the new Mrs. Barbauld. Although they could not have children of their own, she adopted with much delight her nephew Charles, the son of her brother John. It was here that she wrote Early Lessons and Hymns in Prose, created especially for Charles and her other young students.[116] After a while they left Palgrave to travel abroad. They returned to England when her brother became ill and moved to Stoke Newington to care for him. Mrs. Barbauld's life here was not peaceful. Mr. Barbauld's mental illness was degenerating, and the marriage finally ended when he grabbed a knife and pursued his wife around the kitchen table. She narrowly escaped injury only by climbing out the window. Mr. Barbauld was sent to London under the supervision of a caretaker. He escaped and was found dead in the New River in 1808.[117] Mrs. Barbauld grieved her husband's death, and found relief from her sorrows by writing. In 1810 she edited a collection of British novelists, including her own essays and critical reviews.[118] The remainder of her days were spent

---

[115]Anne Katherine Elwood, Memoirs of the Literary Ladies of England, Vol. I (London: Henry Colburn, 1843, reprinted New York: AMS Press, n.d.), p. 238.

[116]Hamilton, Women Writers, p. 73.

[117]Ibid., p. 76.

[118]Ibid., p. 77.

quietly surrounded by her friends. This later writing was confined to her own circle due to the severe criticism she received for a set of poems published late in life. One of her
last works was a poem entitled "Life." The concluding verse
demonstrates both the quality of her writing and her positive
outlook.

> Life! we've been long together
> Through pleasant and through cloudy weather,
> 'Tis hard to part when friends are dear;
> Perhaps 'twill cause a sigh, a tear;
>   Then steal away, give little warning,
>   Choose thine own time;
> Say not good-night, but in brighter chime
> Bid me good-morning.[119]

Mrs. Barbauld was a prominent and well respected member of
the upper middle class intelligentsia. She had close affilia-
tions with the Blue Stockings[120] and was associated with the
leading minds of the day. Her adult writing ranged from the
lyrical to the analytic. Her essays on the abolition of the
slave trade and on public and social worship were acclaimed.[121]
James Fox was amazed "that a woman could exhibit such clearness
and consistency of viewpoints." Sir Walter Scott confessed it
was her public reading of poetry that inspired him "to court
the muse."[122] David Garrick, one of the leading actors of the

---

[119]Wordsworth, after committing this piece to memory, said
that he wished the first two lines were his. Ibid., p. 80.

[120]Darton, Children's Books in England, p. 154.

[121]Austin Allibone, A Critical Dictionary of English Literature: British and American Authors, Vol. I (Philadelphia:
J. B. Lippincott, 1870), p. 114.

[122]Montrose Moses, Children's Books and Reading (New York:
Mitchell Kennerly, 1907), p. 96.

eighteenth century, wrote of her poetry,

> Who lately sung the sweetest lay?
> A woman, woman, woman still I say[123]

Part of this success lay in her commitment to quality which was
instilled when as a young girl she studied the elegant style
and proper technique found in the Augustan writings.[124]

Although her poetry and essays made Mrs. Barbauld enormously popular in her own day, it was her children's books that
have spanned the centuries. Her children's books are good both
for the quality of writing and for the philosophy that under-
lies them. Mrs. Barbauld was particularly astute in understanding the education of the very young. In Hymns in Prose
she mused, "Respect in the infant the future man. Destroy not
in man the rudiments of an angel."[125] In her essay entitled
"Education," Mrs. Barbauld stressed that "the child's character
is formed not by the words and counsel of his parents but
rather by his parents' action and interrelations with others."[126] She had a true respect for the young child, and in
his ability to observe and learn. She also sensed that childhood was broken into distinct stages, the learning of the two
year old is different from the six year old, and this is

[123]Rodgers, Georgian Chronicle, p. 61.

[124]Ibid., p. 30.

[125]This quote was supposedly part of Psalm 10 in Hymns in
Prose for Children. Anonymous, "A Forgotten Children's Book,"
Hibbert Journal 63 (Autumn, 1964), p. 30. Checking the source
in an 1830 copy of Hymns in Prose, this researcher was unable
to find it.

[126]Smith, The History of Children's Literature, p. 377.

---

different from a ten year old. This was highly innovative for the time, since it had not been that long in the past that the child was regarded, not as a separate entity, but rather as a miniature adult.

Her inituitive understanding of the young child's learning helped make her lesson books so successful. Lessons for Children from Two to Three Years Old was first published in 1778. The American market picked it up in 1788 and it was also translated into French. Easy Lessons was published in 1780 and was equally a success.[127] In 1869, Miss Yonge wrote of it in Macmillan Magazine, "'Little Charles' as every household tenderly calls 'Easy Lessons' displaced the earlier 'Cobwebs to Catch Flies' and probably three quarters of the gentry of the three last generations have learned to read by his assistance."[128]

In 1786, Hymns in Prose was published. This is probably her best written work. She wished that the child understand G-d in a concrete fashion. To do this she took the commonplace--scenes, objects, and creatures that the child knew well--and instilled in them a sense of wonder and delight. Although she acknowledged her debt to Sir Isaac Watts,[129] hers was a more gentle, imaginative presentation, leaving out the

---

[127]Meigs claims that this was written for Charles in 1760. Meigs, et al., A Critical History of Children's Literature, p. 75. Since Charles was not adopted until 1775, 76? (when he was about three years old), this date cannot be correct.

[128]Miss Yonge, "Children's Literature of the Last Century," Macmillan Magazine (July 1869): 234.

[129]Mary Thwaite, From Primer to Pleasure in Reading (Boston: The Horn Book, Inc., 1963), p. 55.

Puritan warnings of damnation. This book was committed to memory by many generations of children. So familiar were these
verses, that Mrs. Trimmer had her little Frederick in Fabulous
Histories repeat one of them, knowing full well that the child
reader could easily identify with it.

While living near her ailing brother, the two jointly
wrote Evenings at Home (1792-1796).[130] This was a six volume
work comprised of stories, fables, and lessons. The themes
were many; some were exciting adventure tales, others more
didactic in nature. History, plays, realistic fiction, and
science were also represented. In 1905 Alfred Ainger wrote, "I
undertake to say that those who remember these stories, remember them not as names, but as pictures indelibly impressed upon
their imagination, and as lessons which have become part of
their stock of moral wisdom"[131]--an incredible testimonial
written 113 years after its first publication. Mrs. Barbauld's
writing for children came after she established herself as a
prominent author for adults. Mr. Fox and Dr. Johnson both were
appalled at her "wasting her talents in writing books for children." "Waste indeed!" she replied. "To plant the first idea

---

[130]Although John Aiken co-authored Evenings at Home, it is
Mrs. Barbauld, alone, who was chosen for the biographical
sketch. This is because Mrs. Barbauld is the one who is known
as a major writer of the late eighteenth century children's
didactic school, not her brother. She so overshadowed her
brother in fame and in lasting literary recognition that at
times modern literary historians leave out Dr. Aiken's name
when citing Evenings at Home.

[131]Smith, The History of Children's Literature, p. 106.

in a human mind can be no dishonour to any hand."[132]

Mrs. Barbauld was a brilliant, talented, yet traditional member of the late eighteenth century society. In 1843, Miss Elwood wrote of her, "Mrs. Barbauld was exemplary in every relation of life; as a wife, a sister, and a friend, she was beloved, admired, and esteemed; and she must ever be considered as an ornament both to her sex and to her native land."[133] Moses Montrose suggested that she was one of the female writers who through their force of opinion, and plea for freedom of thought helped in the emancipation of her sex.[134] Montrose seems to have misunderstood the writings and documentary evidence. Mrs. Barbauld reflected very much the attitudes toward women in her day. When Mrs. Montague wrote to her suggesting the establishment of a college for young ladies, Mrs. Barbauld was not impressed. She wrote back that women should gain knowledge in a "quiet and unobserved manner"--and the best learning situation for young ladies is from "conversation with a father, a brother, or a friend."[135] In another context, she wrote, "I am full well convinced that to have a too great fondness for books is little favourable to the happiness of a woman . . . . My situation has been peculiar, and would be no

---

132 Hamilton, *Women Writers*, p. 67.

133 Elwood, *Memoirs of Literary Ladies*, p. 224.

134 Moses, *Children's Books and Reading*, pp. 96-97.

135 Elwood, *Memoirs of Literary Ladies*, pp. 229-230.

rule for others."[136]

Mrs. Barbauld reflected in her life and her writing the attitudes of the late eighteenth century. In the best sense she displayed the graciousness, the positiveness, and the charm characterized by that era. When she died at 82, on March 9, 1825, her epitaph praised her "wit, genius, poetic talent and vigorous understanding."[137] This understanding enabled her to help formulate the growing concept of literature for children and left a legacy of writing from which children for many decades learned and derived enjoyment.

A Biographical Sketch of Mrs. Sarah Kirby Trimmer

Mrs. Sarah Kirby Trimmer was probably the most outspoken and the most important of the didactic children's authors of the late eighteenth century. Her importance lies not only in her writings for children, but also because she was instrumental in helping to establish the Sunday School movement in England. Her untiring efforts in aiding the poor and in striving for educational quality for all, caused her to go beyond the normal boundaries established for women in her day. Yet she, like the others, was not a progressive; her views on the position of women in society, as well as her personal behavior were quite typical. She was a conservative, growing more

---

[136]Patterson, Rousseau's Emile and Early Children's Literature, p. 41.

[137]St. John, ed., The Osbourne Collection of Early Children's Books, p. 108.

extreme in her later years. Her conservative views reflected the new wave of religious revival sweeping over England, and with this, the desire and duty to help the less fortunate. Because of her prolific writing on educational theory, and ultra-conservative reviewing of contemporary children's books, she has come under the strongest attack by twentieth century literary historians and commentators. Much of this commentary is overly critical, often demonstrating a lack of understanding of Mrs. Trimmer's motives and general societal attitudes of the eighteenth century.

Sarah Kirby Trimmer was born at Ipswich on the sixth of January, 1741. She was the only daughter and eldest child of Joshua and Sarah Kirby. Her father was a well respected scholar who authored Method of Perspective Made Easy and The Perspective of Architecture. The success of these books led to his being given the position of tutor to the royal household where he taught the Prince of Wales and Queen Charlotte. Her relationship with her father was a close one which continued throughout their lives. From him, she gained her strong feelings toward religion and virtue, and considered these to be one of the "greatest blessings in life."[138] Under his direction, she not only received training for the usual female accomplishments of her day--English, French, penmanship, and oral reading, but he also guided her reading to Milton, Thomas, and Young, and through his conversations "opened and enlarged her

---

[138]Elwood, Memoirs of Literary Ladies, p. 202.

mind."[139] He encouraged her to study art, where she displayed considerable talent, but only used this skill in entertaining her own children.[140] Through her father, she was introduced to the intellectual leaders of the eighteenth century--Hogarth, Gainsborough, Dr. Gregory Sharp and Dr. Johnson, with all of whom she spent considerable time. Also her father was the first one to recognize her literary talents (as shown in her letter writing) and was the first to seriously suggest that she should begin to write formally.[141]

When the family moved to Kew, she met Mr. Trimmer, "a man of an agreeable person, pleasing manners, and exemplary virtues; about two years older than herself."[142] Mrs. Trimmer loved her husband deeply. Throughout the two volume work of her Life and Writings, she speaks of him tenderly. When he died suddenly, one night, she grieved immensely, and referred often to missing his companionship and counsel. In their life together she bore twelve children, with all but three surviving to adulthood.[143] She was a devoted mother, and as she did with all her endeavors, she threw herself into the role with

---

[139]Ibid., p. 205.

[140]Ibid., p. 203.

[141]Yarde, The Life and Works of Sarah Trimmer, p. 21.

[142]Anonymous. Some Account of the Life and Writings of Mrs. Trimmer, Vol. I (London: F. C. and J. Rivington, 1814), p. 14.

[143]Her son John died at sixteen or so, Annabella suffered a painful death at five or six from a congenital stomach problem, and the tenth child, Decimus, was lost in infancy. Life and Writings of Mrs. Trimmer, Vol. I, p. 55.

intensity and vigor. A letter to a friend reflects the time spent: "I have been, my dear Madame, the mother of twelve children, nine of whom are still living, five daughters and four sons. All my children were nursed by myself; my daughters educated under the paternal roof; my sons chiefly so. For many years, therefore, I could find but little leisure for reading; the needle was my principal occupation when I was not nursing or teaching."[144]

Her commitment to education was a natural outcome of her maternal activities. She obviously studied the educational process of her own children with a critical eye, and despite what she wrote in the above letter, she found time to read extensively books on educational theory and practice. Her involvement was so consuming that she openly confessed one day that she must have worn out the patience of many a visitor with her constant discussion of her views on education.[145] Following the model her father used with her, she had her own children read the classics as well as the modern histories. To augment their reading and fill in any missing subjects she wrote her own stories and lessons for them. Shortly after Mrs. Barbauld's Easy Lessons was published, Mrs. Trimmer was urged by friends to publish her own. Her first book for children was an Easy Introduction to the Knowledge of Nature, 1780?, to which she appended a small sketch of scriptural

---

[144]Life and Writings of Mrs. Trimmer, Vol. I, p. 16.

[145]Montrose Moses, Children's Books and Reading, p. 107.

history.[146] This appendix was soon expanded into a six volume
work entitled Sacred Histories.[147] In rapid succession, she
wrote a series of school textbooks, including a speller and
assorted histories. Many of the history books were accompanied
by a series of prints, representing different historical
events.[148] These were to be hung in the nursery to aid in com-
prehending the subject matter. For this idea, Mrs. Trimmer
publicly acknowledged her indebtedness to Madame de Genles, who
suggested this method of teaching in her Adele et Theodore
which was printed in England in 1787.[149] In 1786, Mrs. Trimmer's most popular children's book, and her only piece of fiction was seen in the bookshops. Fabulous Histories became
enormously successful. Although Mrs. Trimmer's purpose in
writing this book was to teach children about filial devotion,
kindness toward animals, and general Christian concerns, she
succeeded in going beyond this didactic goal. She created a
delightfully animated animal story, and most significantly, a
story written from the child's point of view.[150]

Her writing for children coincided with her interest in

---

[146]Elwood, Memoirs of Literary Ladies, p. 208.

[147]Thwaite, From Primer to Pleasure in Reading, p. 57.

[148]Life and Writings of Mrs. Trimmer, Vol. I, p. 51.

[149]For example, in her Ancient Histories, one volume contains full page prints, each numbered, the other volume labels
each print and gives a written description. Mrs. Trimmer, A
Description of a Set of Prints of Ancient History, 2 vol. (London: Baldwin, Cradock, and Joy, 1821).

[150]Blanch E. Weekes, Literature and the Child (New York:
Silver, Burdett, and Co., 1935), p. 56.

Robert Raikes' Sunday School movement. She quickly became committed and established her own school at Brentford.[151] Mrs. Trimmer felt that too often in the schools of her day, the teaching was mechanical and lifeless, the discipline far too severe. The Charity Spelling Book and her other school texts were specifically written to raise the quality of education.[152] So well known was her work, that in 1787, the Queen summoned her to Windsor Castle for a consultation on Sunday Schools. In the same year she solidified and publicized her views on the subject by writing The Economy of Charity.[153] Her interest and concern for educating the poor continued to grow. "My . . . desire is to see the children of the poor improve in godly knowledge and peace," Mrs. Trimmer wrote in her diary on January 1, 1793.[154] On February 15 in the same year, she continued, "Thou knowest my zeal for thy service, my love for the poor children whom I wish to train in thy faith."[155] She also began writing for the Society for Promoting Christian Knowledge, which disseminated inexpensive educational pamphlets to the poor of all ages.[156]

In the late 1790's, a greater sense of purpose in life

---

[151]Darton, Children's Books in England, p. 160.

[152]Yarde, The Life and Works of Sarah Trimmer, p. 41.

[153]Darton, Children's Books in England, p. 160.

[154]Life and Writings of Mrs. Trimmer, Vol. II, p. 3.

[155]Ibid., p. 17.

[156]Thwaite, From Primer to Pleasure in Reading, p. 57.

seemed to come upon Mrs. Trimmer. She longed for clear minded-
ness, time, and strength to further her writings. "I want to
write something," she mused, "upon bettering the condition of
the poor; in short I have formed plans, I fear beyond my power
to execute."[157] She does not specify exactly what these plans
were. Perhaps they were her establishment of various charity
and industry schools which taught the poor, new skills emerging
out of the Industrial Revolution. Or perhaps it was the writing (and editing)[158] of the Guardian of Education which was
first put on sale in 1802. She began the work "to write a critique on some of the most objectable of [children's] publications; but as books of a dangerous tendency were daily making
their appearance, the idea was suggested of a periodical work,
in which books expressively written upon education should be
examined, as well as those for the use of children, and a general view of the subject be brought forward."[159] This work is
important in the history of education, for it gives a contemporary view of leading eighteenth century educational theorists
and philosophers: Rousseau (Volume I), Locke (Volume I), Edgeworth (Volume II), Hume (Volume II), Pope's "Essay on Man"
(Volume II), Madame de Genles (Volume III) and Dr. Andrew
Bell's study of education in a male asylum (Volume IV). Mrs.

---

[157]Yarde, The Life and Work of Sarah Trimmer, p. 27.

[158]She is often called the editor of The Guardian of Education, although up to this date, this researcher has found no
other contributors other than the previously published excerpts
from books and essays.

[159]Life and Writings of Mrs. Trimmer, Vol. I, p. 57.

Trimmer also pioneered the systematic reviewing of children's
literature in this work.[160]   She categorized the literature into
"Books for Children," "Books for Young Persons," and "School
Books," writing hundreds of reviews.

Despite the magnitude of the Guardian of Education, and
its historical importance, this set of books has in retrospect
hurt Mrs. Trimmer's reputation; and perhaps damaged the re-
spectability of other didactic writers as well.   There is no
question that the views expressed are often ultra conservative.
Mrs. Trimmer was working under a deep moral and religious con-
viction that the young had to be protected against the onslaught of books written for them.   Many of her reviews are
indeed harsh and to our modern eyes, ridiculous.   To the classic, Robinson Crusoe, she gives only a cautious approval and
felt that it should not be given to "all boys without discrimi-
nation, as it might lead to a rambling life and a desire for
adventure."[161]   The reviews most scoffed at by twentieth century historians were her critiques of the fairy tales, especially Cinderella, who was accused of causing all of the worst
human emotions to arise in the child.[162]

It should be noted that in Volume I, Mrs. Trimmer wrote
how she enjoyed the fairy stories as a child.   Only when a letter came in from a reader criticizing her reminiscences, did

---

[160]Thwaite, From Primer to Pleasure in Reading, p. 58.

[161]Trimmer, The Guardian of Education, Vol. II, p. 384.

[162]Ibid., p. 417.

Mrs. Trimmer feel compelled to make such a strong stand. One
wonders if this specific review had not been written, or if The
Guardian of Education had a milder tone, would the criticism of
the didactic school be so harsh today? Even though her standards of book selection and reviewing are not those that we use
today, Mrs. Trimmer was working under the concept that books
are important and should be chosen with judicious care. For
this, she should be remembered with respect.[163]

Mrs. Trimmer continued to work on The Guardian of Education until 1806, when for health reasons she had to stop. She
never fully recovered from the strain.[164] On December 15,
1810, while sitting in the study chair where she did her writing, Sarah Trimmer peacefully died. She was indeed a great
woman of her day. A friend wrote that "she walked with kings,
and worked with the poor."[165] She was a devoted mother, a loving and dutiful wife, a gifted writer, and a woman whose un-
bounded energy was directed to the good of all. In her eulogy,
she was said to be a woman whose "talents and meekness, knowledge and humility were . . . totally blended."[166] This is certainly the picture of a proper late eighteenth century woman.
However after reading her scathing discussions and vehement

---

[163]Judith St. John, "Mrs. Trimmer--Guardian of Education,"
Hornbook 46 (February 1970): 25.

[164]Yarde, The Life and Work of Sarah Trimmer, p. 5.

[165]Ibid., p. 28.

[166]St. John, "Mrs. Trimmer--Guardian of Education," Hornbook (February 1970), p. 28.

rebuttals in The Guardian of Education, one wonders if the word "meek" is appropriate, but it seems that her contemporaries saw her manners and attitudes as "mild and gentle, modest and unassuming."[167] The love and gratitude of those whom she helped was clearly demonstrated by the headstone that was paid for with contributions that poured in from rich and poor alike.[168]

Mrs. Trimmer has been sorely misunderstood by modern critics. She has been thought by some to have been Calvinistic in attitude, viewing the child as naturally sinful, filled with Satanic impulses.[169] This was not the case. To a young teacher she wrote, "Be as lively as you can with your pupils, and endeavor to make the important things appear in an engaging light to them."[170] These are not the words of a reactionary, or a throwback to Puritanical teachings. Rather they are the sentiments of a woman who understood the nature of children and the process of learning. For her work, especially in promoting quality education for all, we should be indebted.

Eighteenth Century Conceptualizations of Childhood and Child Rearing Practices

In 1929, Arthur Groom was quoted as saying, "To write for children, you must be prepared to be their humble and obedient

---

[167]Ibid., p. 25.

[168]Yarde, The Life and Work of Sarah Trimmer, p. 29.

[169]Percy Muir, English Children's Books from 1600-1900 (New York: Frederick A. Praeger, 1954), pp. 84-85.

[170]Life and Writings of Mrs. Trimmer, Vol. II, p. 303.

servant, to obey, not to command."[171] Implied in this statement is a very modern conceptualization of childhood: To be
successful with children one must be their devoted follower,
gamboling with them through sunlit meadow and asphalt playground, dancing to the elusive Pied Piper's tune. The image is
indeed a romantic one, and for us very comprehensible. We live
in an age where childhood is considered very special, a time
doted upon and extended. Children today are unique, set apart
from the rest of society with their own physicians, a whole
variety of specialized pedagogues to teach them through their
various developmental stages, their own specialty shops for
clothing, haircutting, toys, etc., and their own amusements.
However, if Mr. Groom had dared to venture such a statement in
a previous era, it would have been considered by the more liberal as balderdash, by the extremists as heresy. For before
the seventeenth century the child was seen as a miniatrue
adult, not as an individual within a special stage of development. The very young were seen almost as defective, and were
basically ignored until they reached the age of six or seven
when they could engage in adult society.[172] It was not until

---

[171]Lillian Smith, The Unreluctant Years (New York: Viking
Press, 1953), p. 13.

[172]In Centuries of Childhood, Philippe Aries tells horrif-
ic stories of infants being used as balls in tossing games, by
medieval courtiers. Montaigne comments in the sixteenth century, "I have lost two or three children in infancy, not without regret, but without much sorrow." To lose one's children
with only "regret" seems callous, but to be uncertain of the
number of offspring seems inconceivable. Lawrence Stone in The
Family, Sex and Marriage in England 1500-1800 (New York: Harper and Row, 1979) suggests one of the major factors causing

the seventeenth century that children were thought of as being special in themselves, and a conceptualization of childhood emerged. Children were now dressed in clothes stylistically different from the adult fashion, they had their own games and toys, and were given special attention. They were now cared for deliberately and purposefully. Parents began to enjoy their children; play with them as children rather than as peers, and grew seriously concerned with the child's moral development and welfare. A monitoring of the young began which had not been seen before. The children were subjected "to a thoughtful and rigorous regime designed to inculcate self-control, to shield them from the immodesties of adult life, and [treated] with seriousness and respect." The concept of childhood was also extended past infancy to include the years up through early adolescence.[173] This changing attitude toward childhood was due to multiple factors. In the 1600's, infant mortality dropped, allowing the parent the freedom, psychologically, to invest love and time in the very young. Contraception also came into use. The fertility rate dropped making new additions to the family more welcome.[174] The social fabric of

---

this disregard of young children was the enormously high infant mortality rate. To invest "too much emotional capital in such ephemeral beings" was psychologically unsound.

[173] D. Hunt, "The Historical Background: Philippe Areis and the Evolution of the Family," from a collection of articles gathered for a course at Ben-Gurion University, Beersheva, Israel, 1978, p. 35.

[174] Lloyde de Mause, ed., The History of Childhood (New York: Psychohistory Press, 1974), p. 363.

the society was also changing. Small nuclear families were developing, much different from the larger clans and extended kinship groups of the medieval era. This new concept of the family was inseparable from the developing conceptualization of childhood. Closer relationships with children emerged and with it a desire to provide the offspring with safe, well regulated living space.[175]

Two views of childhood emerged simultaneously in the seventeenth century. One was the Puritan's, which saw the child as inherently evil, born "full of the stains and pollutions which it inherits from our first parents through our loins."[176] It was therefore necessary to educate the child in a way to protect him from his own self destruction, and subdue his bestial nature. Child rearing practices were harsh; to beat the devil out of the child was accepted literally. The opposing view can be seen by Bishop Earle's statement in 1628, "A child is a man in a small letter, yet the best copy of Adam before he tasted of Eve or the apple . . . . His soul is a white paper unscribbled with observations of the world . . . . He is purely happy because he knows no evil."[177] This was a more compassionate, gentler approach. The essential goodness of the child would triumph over the bad, if the child was given the

---

[175]Hunt, "The Historical Background," p. 36.

[176]J. H. Plumb, "The New World in Eighteenth-Century England," Past and Present 67 (1974): 67.

[177]Alice Law, "The Cult of the Child-spirit in Modern Literature," Transactions of the Royal Society of Literature of the United Kingdom, second series, 33 (1915), reprint ed. (Kraus Reprint, 1970), p. 126.

correct environment and proper education. As William Penn advised parents, "love them with wisdom, correct them with affection, never strike in passion, and suit the corrections to their ages as well as the fault."[178]

When John Locke began his educational writings at the end of the seventeenth century, they were immediately accepted, and he was heralded as the leading spokesman on education and child rearing of the day. This was not because his ideas were innovative or novel, but rather because they reflected the "microcosm of English domesticity."[179] The Puritans were falling from power, both politically and in physical numbers. The more benign child rearing practices advocated by Bishop Earle, John Evelyn, William Penn and others were currently in practice. Locke eloquently and clearly compiled these ideas, extending them, and adding specific suggestions. The end result was Thoughts Concerning Education which became the bible on child rearing practices. This treatise very much was affected by the Age of Reason, for Locke developed a tradition of education based on the best and fastest way to create rational adults out of immature children. Using the model of the child as a tabula rasa, Locke demonstrated step by step how to fill this blank sheet of paper with the proper habits.

Unlike his Puritan predecessors who advised a cool, distant parent-child relationship, and maintaining obedience

---

[178] Stone, The Family, Sex and Marriage in England, p. 274.

[179] Darton, Children's Books in England, p. 112.

through force, Locke stressed training for understanding.
"Keep the mind in an easy calm Temper when you would have it
receive your Instructions or any Increase of knowledge," wrote
Locke, "Tis impossible to draw fair and regular characters on a
trembling mind as on a shaking paper."[180] Only with the very
young, "too tender to be reasoned with" should force be used.[181]
Psychological manipulation rather than physical coercion should
be used in maintaining discipline. Rewards used as incentives
were suggested, rather than accentuating the wrongdoings by
whippings. Locke stressed that the child's interest toward
learning be awakened through play and pleasant methods of instruction. "Thus children may be cozened into a knowledge of
their letters . . . and play themselves into what others are
whipped for."[182] Physical exercise and proper health habits
were advocated. Locke also gave mothers very practical suggestions on proper diet, manner of dress, feeding and sleeping
schedules, and toilet training. One of the important points
Locke makes in the book deals with respect for the child. If
the father "would have his son have a respect for him and his
orders, [the parent] himself [must have] a great reverence for
the son."[183]

---

[180]Gesiena Andreae, The Dawn of Juvenile Literature in
England (Amsterdam: H. J. Paris, 1925), p. 10.

[181]Plumb, "The New World in Eighteenth-Century England,"
Past and Present 67: 67.

[182]Thwaite, From Primer to Pleasure in Reading, p. 32.

[183]Stone, The Family, Sex and Marriage in England, p. 259.

The impact of Thoughts Concerning Education was enormous.
With his push for pleasant education and learning through play,
Locke set the stage for the publishing of children's books that
were amusing and appropriate to the child's level. Thomas
Boreman, one of the first publishers of children's books,
echoed the Lockean philosophy in the preface of Gigantik Histories (1740-1743), "During the Infant-age every busy and always enquiring, there is no fixing of the mind, but by amusing
it."[184]   The advertisement for Mary Cooper's The Child's New
Play-Thing (1743) read:

> The Child's Plaything
> I recommend for cheating
> Children into learning
> Without any Beating[185]

The great John Newbery also listened to Locke's words when pre-
paring his manuscripts. Not only did he publicly acknowledge
Locke by name in some of the prefaces[186] but his characters
also reflected Locke's theory. Miss Margery, of Goody Two
Shoes fame, taught reading to the village children by using
alphabet blocks and other little games. It should be noted
that although these early children's writers most probably
agreed with Lockean philosophy, they were also aware that it
was this educational theory that was most adhered to by the

---

[184]Thomas Boreman, The Gigantic History of Two Famous
Giants and other Curiosities in Guildhall, London. 1740-1743
(reprint ed., New York: Garland Publishers, 1977), n.p.

[185]Children's Literature, Vol. I (Philadelphia: Temple
University Press, 1972), p. 47.

[186]Ibid., p. 48.

purchasing public--the parents.

There is no question that the late eighteenth century didactic writers were also influenced by Locke's theory of child
rearing and his conceptualization of childhood. They demonstrated a great respect for the child, certainly tried to make
their teachings enjoyable, banished the rod, and stressed
reason.

But as demonstrated before, the second half of the eighteenth century was fraught with changes in societal attitudes
and mores. Child rearing practices would naturally be affected
by such changes. Stone hypothesizes that at this time there
were no less than four distinct concepts of childhood in opera-
tion, these in turn produced different child rearing practices.[187] Locke's theory, although probably the most widely
accepted, was just one of them. It is interesting that his was
most closely aligned with the changes wrought by the pre-
industrial revolution. Through experimentation and study,
things could be created to produce a better way of life. Anal-
ogously, the child as seen by Locke was open and malleable.
Through the proper education and experiences, the child could
be shaped into a productive member of society. The child rearing techniques that came from Locke's theories stressed sobri-
ety, obedience, industry, thrift, benevolence and compassion--
all suitable goals for the industrializing of Britain.[188] A

---

[187]Stone, The Family, Sex and Marriage in England, p. 255.

[188]Plumb, "The New World in Eighteenth-Century England,"
Past and Present 67: 67.

purposefulness of life was stressed. "Of idleness comes no good, but of all labour there is some profit," said John Barnard to his congregation in 1737. Eleazer Moody advised children, "Let thy Countenance be moderately chearful, neither laughing nor Frowning. Laugh not aloud, but silently smile upon occasion."[189] Proper decorum was strictly regulated.

Yet Locke's pleas for a gentler, more compassionate approach to children, rid the 1700's of the stern formality seen in parent-child relations of the previous century. The reserved "Madam" and "Sir" were replaced with the more affectionate "Mama" and "Papa." Children were no longer required to remain standing or kneel in the presence of their parents. The parents in turn developed pet names for their offspring, referring to their little ones as "tender plants," "little lambs," "my choicest plants." Implied in these terms of endearment was that children needed to be protected, carefully tended and "cultivated."[190] They were to be nurtured and educated so that they could be effective members of the newly made aggressive, commercial society.[191]

A second prevalent conceptualization of childhood in the eighteenth century was fueled by the religious revival and the

---

[189]Monica Kiefer, American Children through their Books: 1700-1835 (Philadelphia: University of Pennsylvania Press, 1948), p. 73.

[190]de Mause, ed., The History of Childhood, p. 363.

[191]J. H. Plumb, Foreword to Early Children's Books and Their Illustrations: Pierpont-Morgan Library, by Gerald Gottlieb (Boston: David R. Godine, 1975), p. xviii.

teachings of John Wesley. This conservative movement resur-
rected the older Puritan view that the child was born infused
with original sin. Only through suppression of his will and
total subordination to those in authority could the child's
bestial nature be curbed and he could achieve everlasting salvation. Following the literal interpretation of the Bible,
they picked up the rod once again. Wesley insisted that parents must "break the will of the child, to bring his will into
subjection to yours, that it may be afterwards subject to the
will of God." Hannah More wrote in 1799, it is a "fundamental
error to consider children as innocent beings . . . rather
[they are] beings who bring into the world a corrupt nature and
evil disposition."[192]

This harsh Calvinistic approach was also subscribed to by
the lower classes, not because of religious beliefs but rather
because they were relatively unaffected by changes in societal
attitudes. They were simply following the model established by
their own parents.[193] A third conceptualization arose from a
small group of astrology worshippers. They felt that the po-
tentialities and character of the child was determined by the
position of the stars and astrological signs. Therefore neither education nor environment could either form good habits or
restrain bad ones. This in a sense is oddly reminiscent of the
predeterministic view of child development that would emerge in

---

[192]Stone, The Family, Sex and Marriage in England, p. 294.

[193]Ibid., p. 293.

the late nineteenth century and come into prominence in the
early part of this century.

The conceptualization of childhood that had the most profound impact upon subsequent generations and was popular at the
time, emerged with the publication of Emile by Jean Jacques
Rousseau. This book has been seen by some as "one of the most
seminal books in the history of literature."[194] In England
alone, it influenced some 200 publications before the close of
the eighteenth century.[195] In the preface, Rousseau denied the
tabula rasa model of the child as well as the Puritan's view of
the child as innately sinful. "We know nothing of childhood,"
Rousseau wrote, "and with our mistaken notions the further we
go astray. The wisest writers . . . are always looking for the
man in the child, without considering what he is before he becomes a man."[196] The child was not an empty vessel to be
filled, but rather a distinct entity; good by nature, born with
certain capabilities which should be nurtured. Rousseau, much
more so than Locke, placed within the child a specialness, and
gave to the whole concept of childhood, a romantic view. The
child's actions are naturally moral, bad habits and vice are
learned from exposure to adult society. Let the child be the

---

[194] Barbara Kaye Greenleaf, Children Through the Ages (New York: McGraw Hill, 1978), p. 65.

[195] Ibid., p. 64.

[196] Lynne Merle Rosenthal, "The Child Informed: Attitudes Toward the Socialization of the Child in the Nineteenth Century English Children's Literature" (Ph.D. dissertation, Columbia University, 1974), p. 32.

child, he pleaded, before he becomes a man. Rousseau was also keenly aware of the historical changes of his era. He wanted not to create the productive citizen, but rather a man adaptable to a changing world. To survive, man must be attuned, according to Rousseau, to the "immediate responses of natural man, of the savage, who tied to no one place or tradition, must continually discover the motives and consequences of his actions for himself." Man must "feel with his heart."[197]

Rousseau's chief aim was to bring up the child according to his own laws of nature; education should be dictated by the child's own interests. Formal education was discredited. Rousseau wrote: "A child needs no other teacher than experience, no school-room but the open country which is also his playground; all that the tutor need to do is to enter into his interests and amusements as an equal, and watch over him while he educates himself."[198] The only intrusion into this natural system was to set up learning situations which would develop self reliance. The role of the tutor was carefully defined. He was never to scold or give out harsh punishments. Discipline was to be maintained through natural consequences. He was to guide only, never give orders or be too restrictive. "Well conditioned liberty" was to be the end result.[199] Physical exercise was to play an important part in the child's

---

[197]Ibid., p. 31.

[198]Bertha E. Mahoney, ed., Realms of Gold in Children's Books (New York: Doubleday, Dorant and Co., 1929), pp. 9-10.

[199]Rosenthal, "The Child Informed" (Ph.D. dissertation, Columbia University, 1974), p. 38.

education up to the pre-adolescent stage,[200] since the child up to this point did not have the ability to reason. Therefore, Rousseau maintained books were of little use for him. (He was adamantly opposed to the children's literature of his day and the only book he felt suitable was Robinson Crusoe.) When the child reached the age of twelve, reasoning developed and a more formal training period could begin.

Reaction to Emile was immediate, translations appeared as soon as the French edition came out in 1762.[201] Many applauded his recommendations for close mother-child relations, sensible punishments, and the development of self-reliance. In equal numbers, disapproval came. His striking out of class distinctions was too revolutionary for some.[202] The church was outraged at the total lack of religious training. For others, the emphasis of feeling over reason was simply inconceivable. Few however realized the most revolutionary part of his theses--the period of childhood is a special time, important in its own right.[203]

---

[200]In Emile, Rousseau describes the stages of childhood:
infancy to two years--the child to all purposes is still an
    animal;
two to twelve years--the child is dominated by his senses;
pre-adolescent years from twelve to fifteen--the child can now
    reason and learn more formally. Books are used in teaching.
    Ethics and morality are brought into the curriculum.

[201]Rosenthal, "The Child Informed" (Ph.D. dissertation, Columbia University, 1974), p. 59.

[202]Andreae, The Dawn of Juvenile Literature in England, p. 68.

[203]Greenleaf, Children Through the Ages, p. 63.

Rousseau's influence on contemporary children's literature was also great. Thomas Day's Sandford and Merton was a deliberate effort to put Rousseau's philosophy into a children's book. The omnipresent tutor sprang up in countless volumes guiding the children through the meadow to study the pollen collection of bees, and down to the stream to investigate the physical properties of wind and water. Rousseau himself gave suggestions on writing a proper children's book. "Make up tales, make up fables from which [the child] can draw his own moral conclusions and which he can turn to his own personal use . . . proceed from things he may have observed himself."[204] His influence upon child rearing techniques was equally profound. Discipline was begun to be seen as an interference, injurious to the development of the child's character.[205] "Why need a child's will be broken," wrote a Moravian contemporary, "The difference between strength of will and weakness of will is often the difference between efficiency and inefficiency."[206]

As a result of this, an extremely permissive child rearing style became fashionable, particularly in the upper classes.

---

[204]Isabelle Jan, On Children's Literature (London: Bayles and Sons, 1973), p. 23.

[205]Stone hypothesizes what partly influenced Rousseau and this progressive child rearing model was also the growing interest in the individual and the demand for personal autonomy. With this came the "recognition that it is morally wrong to make exaggerated demands for obedience, or to manipulate or coerce the individual beyond a certain point in order to achieve social or political ends." Stone, The Family, Sex and Marriage in England, p. 151.

[206]Keefer, American Children Through Their Books, p. 85.

Mrs. Sherwood, a didactic writer who was popular in the early nineteenth century, noted this when visiting a friend. The son, who was quite a big boy, was lolling about the floor. When asked by his mother to arise and greet the visitor he retorted with "I won't or I shan't!" Mrs. Sherwood was not particularly surprised at this lack of decorum, for she said, "I have lived to see this single specimen multiplied beyond calculation."[207] Another eyewitness account tells of the home of Admiral and Mrs. Graves, whose children were never contradicted and never had their hair cut. "When three or four of them cry at once for the same thing and run tearing and screaming around the room together with their long tails, the effect on strangers is rather surprising."[208] With such permissiveness in early childhood, the result at times can lead to a general lack of respect toward parents and/or conventions at a later age. One eighteenth century father's lament about just this, is oddly reminiscent of the cry of American parents in the 1960's. A Mr. Fox implored his son to get his hair cut "to a reasonable and gentlemanlike shortness . . . [the way] Eton boys wear it . . . . It is effeminate, it is ugly, and it must be inconvenient."[209]

This excessive permissiveness was not without critics. In one parent manual, the author spoke of a "growing degeneracy"

---

[207]Stone, The Family, Sex and Marriage in England, p. 276.

[208]Ibid., p. 277.

[209]Rosamond Bayne-Powell, The English Child in the Eighteenth Century (New York: E. P. Dutton and Co., 1939), p. 2.

among the young, and warned against "too great remissness in parents and governors of families." He concluded that "most of the evils that abound among us proceed from the defects of family government."[210] The Edgeworths expressed disapproval of the growing indulgence of parents toward children, "particularly the waste of money on useless toys."[211] James Nelson, Richard Costeke, and others wrote pamphlets warning that this type of child rearing practice would only lead to degeneration and ruin.[212]

Oddly enough, coming from this same philosophy was another child rearing practice; that of "hardening" the child to make him more self-reliant and more adaptable. Certainly Rousseau's "Noble Savage" did without the comforts of life, likewise the children could live a more spartan existence. Harsh regimes were imposed upon the children, particularly the little girls. Rousseau believed that women must "early be accustomed to restraint" in order to prepare them for the "yoke of propriety," the strictest and "most enduring of restraints."[213] One little girl, every morning was dipped into a tub of the coldest well water. Her brother said of this practice, "I cannot remember

---

[210]de Mause, ed., The History of Childhood, p. 373.

[211]Plumb, "The New World in Eighteenth-Century England," Past and Present 67: 93.

[212]Stone, The Family, Sex and Marriage in England, p. 377.

[213]Rosenthal, "The Child Informed" (Ph.D. dissertation, Columbia University, 1974), p. 54.

having seen it without horror."[214] The girls were put in heavy
iron collars and iron stays to keep their backs straight, at
times even suspended from the ceilings or placed in stocklike
contraptions. One governess pinned a bunch of thistle thorns
to the collar of her little charge's pinafore, in order to
teach her to keep her chin up.[215]

Despite some of the cruelties imposed on children in the
name of Rousseau, this new method of child rearing had for the
most part positive effects. The permissiveness developed individuals less prone to violence, and more capable of personal
attachments. One serious drawback, however, was limited parental restraint, and not teaching the children to comply with societal rules. Without a sense of restraint and understanding
the importance of society's dictates and mores, parents were
failing to prepare their children for the adult world--an
essential process in the socialization of the child.[216]

Even with Locke's philosophy of treating the child with
respect and Rousseau's concept of the special quality of childhood itself, many parents had not yet incorporated these ideals
into their day to day interaction with the young. J. H. Plumb
maintains that there were still "dark and lowering clouds . . . .

---

[214]Bayne-Powell, The English Child in the Eighteenth Century, p. 7.

[215]Elizabeth Godfrey, English Children in the Olden Times
(London: Methuen and Co., 1907), p. 258.

[216]Stone, The Family, Sex and Marriage in England, p. 284.

Children, in fact had become objects."[217] "In a sense they had become superior pets--sometimes spoilt excessively . . . sometimes treated with indifference or even brutality, but usually, as with pets betwixt and between."[218] The children were used to both demonstrate and further their parents' social aspirations. Probably more for the parents' status than for the child's enjoyment, enormous sums of money were spent on extravagant gilt toys. Early precocity was stressed, teaching children as young as two and three to read. Mrs. Hartley wrote to Sir William Pepys about this: "Education is the rage of the times. Everybody tries to make their children more wonderful than any children of their acquaintances. The poor little things are so crammed with knowledge that there is scant time for them to obtain . . . exercise, and play."[219]

The children of the poor were given even less regard than their more wealthy age-mates. Captain Thomas Coran, returning to Britain after a lengthy stay abroad was appalled at the sight of abandoned and dying infants in the streets of London.[220] Those that survived infancy were herded into the new factories to work fourteen to sixteen hours a day under terrible conditions. Others were shoved up chimneys to sweep and

---

[217]Plumb, "The New World in Eighteenth-Century England," Past and Present 67: 93.

[218]Plumb, Foreword to Early Children's Books and Their Illustration, by Gerald Gottlieb, p. xxix.

[219]Repplier, A Happy Half Century and Other Essays, p. 139.

[220]Greenleaf, Children Through the Ages, p. 72.

clean away the soot and debris. This was perhaps the most hor-
rific of all child jobs. Standing in black, narrow flues,
their bones became deformed, and many suffered from a painful
disease called "chimney sweep's cancer."[221]

But it must be remembered that overall there was a re-
markable and positive change in the attitudes regarding children in eighteenth century England. The most important one was
the warmth and tenderness that developed in the parent-child
relationship. This crossed class barriers and was obviously
seen in all aspects of life. A German gentleman, traveling in
Britain in 1783, remarked, "Parents here, in general, nay even
those of the lower classes seem to be kind and indulgent to
their children."[222] There was also an active attempt on the
part of adults to become better parents. Between 1750 and
1814, some 2,400 "how-to" manuals were published, informing
parents of the newest educational theories and child rearing
strategies.[223] One reason for this influx was the greater
awareness that children are special, different from adults and
perhaps the children needed specialized care. Another stems
from the very practical concerns of the upwardly mobile middle
class. The pre-industrial revolution propelled changes in social status. The nouveau riche, in particular, needed and
wanted to know how to train their children to be proper members

---

[221]Ibid., p. 74.

[222]R. B. Morgan, ed., Readings in English Social History
(Cambridge: Cambridge University Press, 1923), p. 522.

[223]Stone, The Family, Sex and Marriage in England, p. 258.

of their new class. The tried and true method of teaching your children in the same manner your parents trained you, was no longer satisfactory.

Also, with the new wave of humanism, coupled with the growing respect of the child, legislation was sought to protect children from detrimental working conditions. The first child labor law was enacted in 1788, prohibiting the use of children under eight from working in factories. Foundling hospitals were established to care for abandoned children. The number of schools increased, providing rich and poor alike, more opportunities for education.

The British child of the late eighteenth century was far more fortunate than his predecessors in the Puritan era and the middle ages. He was treated with far more compassion, far more love. Yet, he was still viewed much differently than our modern child. The romantic notion of the innocence and beauty of childhood, first formulated by Rousseau, needed another hundred years or so to come into force. This concept blossomed in the late Victorian era and early twentieth century. The children's books by Dodgson, Greenaway, Caldecott, Potter, Barrie, and others reflected this romantic ideal. The children's writers of the late eighteenth century were working under a more "sensible" and "rational" approach to childhood. The Age of Reason was still strongly entrenched in the adult minds. The need to produce individuals to further the strides of the industrial revolution and the new humanism, spawned by the religious revivals and other factors, were undoubtedly operating as they

wrote. The ideal child, which Mrs. Trimmer and the other didactic authors were trying to form, can be seen in Wordsworth's
poem, "The Prelude" (1805):

> Not blind is he
> To the broad follies of the licensed world,
> Yet innocent himself withal, though shrewd,
> And can read lectures upon innocence,
> A miracle of scientific lore,
> Ships he can guide upon the pathless sea,
> And tell you all their cunning; he can read
> The inside of the earth and spell the stars,
> Can string you names of districts, cities, towns,
> The whole world over . . .

The eighteenth century child was precocious, knowledgeable and
benevolent. However, he was deliberately shielded from one important aspect of childhood. Wordsworth eloquently laments
this loss in the same poem.

> Meanwhile old granddam earth is sad to find
> The playthings which her love designed for him
> Unthought of; . . .
> Oh! give us once again the wishing-cap
> Of Fortunatus and the invisible coat
> Of Jack the Giant-Killer, Robin Hood,
> And Sabra in the forest with Saint George

The child would have to patiently wait for another era to let
his fancy and imagination run free.

Thus, the time was ripe for a didactic children's literature to emerge in England in the late eighteenth century. The
didactic nature of this literature is perfectly understandable.
The time was becoming increasingly conservative, spurred on by
religious revivals, fear of the anarchy demonstrated in the
French revolution, a reaction against the decadence of the
first part of the century, and the dramatic changes brought on
by the pre-industrial and agricultural revolutions. Also, the
Age of Reason was still a major component determining social

attitudes--frivolity and fantasy were not acceptable in children's reading material.

The moral overtones of the books also gave the authors a greater legitimacy. As respectable middle class women in the late eighteenth century, Mesdames Trimmer and Barbauld, Miss Edgeworth, and the Kilners had to remain within the narrow confines of society's expectations for women. By writing stories that would teach children to become productive and contented future members of society, they fulfilled societal demands that women should reach out helping and guiding those weaker or less fortunate than themselves, always in a demure and unobtrusive fashion. But their little books were more than just teaching devices. Through their talents and intuitive understanding of children, these authors added a new dimension to stories for the young, and further promoted the developing genre of children's literature.

CHAPTER III

ANALYSIS OF THE REPRINTING DATA OF THE
FIVE SELECTED BOOKS

Introduction

There are few opportunities to appraise contemporary popularity of historical books unless they are classics. Once a
book has fallen from favor, due to outdated theme, weak style,
or some other consideration, the responses from its readers
usually are not investigated. A number of factors may cause
this lack of interest. Critics tend to study why the book has
been "forgotten"--its negative characteristics, rather than
trying to ascertain why the book was once popular. This type
of research can present, however, a very narrow view. Historical importance of the book is overlooked, as well as an understanding of the time period from whence the book emerged.
Another reason why little time is spent in researching responses is the paucity of actual documentary evidence. Discus-
ions in letters and diaries might contain comments referring to
leisure readings, but with the passage of time much of this
material is often lost or destroyed.

The problem of locating such material becomes even more
difficult when dealing with books written for children. Children, due to their inclinations, interest, and lack of critical
writing skills, have produced even fewer such documents. In

the late eighteenth century the problem is further compounded,
for the child would not often write about books read for enjoyment. This was the Age of Reason, where frivolity was frowned
upon and child precocity stressed. The child living in the
late 1700's would more readily write about school texts and
philosophical treatises, for this would be what was expected of
him, and be most apt to please the adult. Discussions on
pleasure reading would be kept to a minimum. An example of
this was found in the 1771-1772 diary of young Lucy Sheldon.
She listed the books she read, but added no comment.[1]

"Eye Witness" Accounts and Contemporary and Near Contemporary Literary Criticism

Two types of eye witness accounts will be discussed in
this section. One group of responses analyzed are those which
were made retrospectively by adults, musing about their own
childhood readings. The other group are the actual accounts of
children reacting to the books. One such piece of documentation found was an episode recounted by a contemporary of Maria
Edgeworth.   While attending a party together, it was reported
that a little girl ran up to Miss Edgeworth and exclaimed, "I
like Simple Susan best!" and then overwhelmed with embarrass-
ment, quickly retreated.[2] For a little girl brought up at the

---

[1]Rosalie V. Halsey, Forgotten Books of the American Nursery: A History of the Development of the American Story-Book
(Boston: Charles E. Goodspeed and Co., 1911), p. 82.

[2]Isabel Clarke, Maria Edgeworth: Her Family and Friends
(London: Hutchinson and Co., n.d.), p. 42.

turn of the nineteenth century, this was indeed an unusual act of temerity. Another child response found was a comment made by a four year old to his mother in the early 1800's.

> Tell Miss Edgeworth I do really think that Rosa-
> mond [the character made famous in "The Purple
> Jar," originally published in The Parent's Assis-
> tant] was foolish not to choose the shoes, but
> her Mama made her go without them very long. I
> would not have made her go barefoot more than a
> week.[3]

This precocious young gentleman seemed to have been very in-volved with the story. A nine year old, in the same time peri-od, made this critical appraisal of Maria Edgeworth's work. "Really that is a very useful as well as an entertaining book."[4]

In a letter written on February 21, 1812, an American boy visiting England describes to his mother the children's books he has encountered. "They have . . . Miss Edgeworth's Parent's Assistant and Moral Tales,[5] with several volumes of Mrs. Bar-bauld's Evenings at Home."[6] In the prolific records of the Edgeworths, it was noted that Evenings at Home was read at the family estate.[7] Another example was found in a letter written by an American, Mrs. Josiah Quincy, in the early nineteenth

---

[3]P. H. Newby, Maria Edgeworth (Denver: Alan Swallow, 1951), p. 37.

[4]Amy Cruse, The Englishman and His Books in the Early Nineteenth Century (New York: Benjamin Blom, 1968), p. 32.

[5]Moral Tales by Maria Edgeworth was a collection of chil-dren's stories, written in much the same way as The Parent's Assistant.

[6]Cruse, The Englishman and His Books, p. 214.

[7]Ibid., p. 214.

century. Writing to a friend in Boston, she requested <u>Moral</u>
<u>Tales</u> by Maria Edgeworth, "If the book can be obtained in one
of the bookstores, if not borrow one . . . and I will replace
it with a new copy." This mother seemed intent upon receiving
a copy for her children, since she added that the sender should
cut the pages from the bindings if necessary.[8]

Nineteenth century adult recollections of their childhood
pleasure reading can also be considered in looking for evidence
of contemporary popularity of a book. This type of documentation, however, is not as pure as an "eye witness" account of
the child himself. One does not know if the recollections are
shaded by the adult's educational and/or child rearing philosophies. Also, since the comments found were given by relatively
prominent persons, it might be the case that they were careful
in their choice of recollections. It is doubtful that they
would mention books scandalous or even questionable in nature.
To the credit of the books selected for this study, the comments made are quite positive. Therefore it could be assumed
that these five selected books were considered respectable examples of children's literature.

In Chapter I in this manuscript, Miss Yonge's delightful
comments on <u>Perambulations of a Mouse</u>, <u>Fabulous Histories</u>, and
<u>Evenings at Home</u> are given (p. 13). In the same chapter, Mr.
Welsh's collected recollections of <u>Fabulous Histories</u>, Miss
Edgeworth's stories, and <u>Evenings at Home</u> are listed (p. 14).

---

[8]Halsey, <u>Forgotten Books of the American Nursery</u>, pp.
158-159.

Alfred Ainger's comments on Evenings at Home are given in Chapter II (p. 62). Robert Louis Stevenson wrote that his father used to read to him from the Parent's Assistant.[9] Florence Nightingale owned an 1802 copy of Maria Edgeworth's Moral Tales[10] and one of Mrs. Trimmer's textbooks.[11] Harriet Martineau reflected in the nineteenth century, "In those days we learned Mrs. Barbauld's Prose Hymns by heart; and there were parts of them which I dearly loved."[12]

Another way to assess contemporary popularity of forgotten books is to peruse contemporary and near contemporary literary reviews. Locating such reviews, like finding eyewitness accounts, also poses problems. Also, the reviews were written by adults, biased by the current child rearing theories and personal philosophic beliefs. Although they do not show the actual response of the reading public, they do give a valid indication of how literary experts assessed the books. In a 1796 critique of Parent's Assistant, which came out immediately after its initial publication, the review is extremely positive.

> In the valuable list of useful books for children, these little volumes will be entitled to a very

[9] Clarke, Maria Edgeworth, p. 33.

[10] Judith St. John, The Osbourne Collection of Early Children's Books: 1566-1910 (Toronto: Toronto Public Library, 1958), p. 248.

[11] Ibid., p. 174.

[12] Betsey Rodgers, Georgian Chronicle: Mrs. Barbauld and Her Family (London: Methuen and Co., 1958), p. 73. Although Hymns in Prose (Prose Hymns) and Moral Tales are not two of the five selected books, contemporary comments have been included to note that the selected authors in this study were known and read.

> distinguished place. They contain a series of
> amusing and interesting tales, happily adapted to
> impress on young minds principles of wisdom and
> sentiments of virtue . . . the stories are in-
> vented with great ingenuity . . . . The author's
> taste, in this class of writing, appears to have
> been formed on the best models; and the work will
> not discredit a place on the same shelf with
> Berquin's Child's Friend, Mrs. Barbauld's Lessons
> for Children, and . . . Evenings at Home. The
> story of Lazy Lawrence is one of the best lec-
> tures on industry which we have ever read.[13]

In the January 1797 issue of Critical Review, the Parent's

Assistant was again highly praised. "The present production is

particularly sensible and judicious; the stories are well writ-

ten, simple, and affecting; calculated, not only for moral ap-

provement, but to exercise the best affections of the human

heart."[14]

Mrs. Trimmer, in her countless reviews in The Guardian of

Education, carefully reviewed the works of Miss Edgeworth, Mrs.

Barbauld and the Kilners. She enthusiastically reviewed Mrs.

Barbauld's and the Kilner's writings. She was more reserved in

her lengthy commentary on The Parent's Assistant. Although

Mrs. Trimmer agreed that the stories were "interesting and

amusing"[15] and the moral overtones eminently proper for chil-

dren, she never gave her wholehearted approval. One reason for

this could be that Practical Education lacked religious

---

[13]"The Parent's Assistant, by Maria Edgeworth, A Review,"
The Monthly Review 21 (Sept. 1796): 89.

[14]Austin Dobson, "The Parent's Assistant," A reprint from
DeLibris Prose and Verse (London: Macmillan, 1911), ed., Lance
Salway, Signal 17 (May 1975): 99.

[15]Mrs. Trimmer, Guardian of Education, Vol. II (London: J.
Hatchard, 1803), p. 357.

teaching, and it was a well known fact that The Parent's Assistant was written to accompany this theoretical text. Mrs. Trimmer came out with public disapproval of Practical Education, therefore, her nitpicking review of these stories is understandable (from her viewpoint). Her review of Evenings at Home was unqualifiedly positive. In the beginning of the seventeen page review she quoted from an important contemporary text, Systems of Education.

> This [Evenings at Home] is one of the best books
> for young children, from seven to ten years old,
> that has yet appeared in the world. The mixture
> of scientific and moral lessons is so happily
> blended . . . [these stories] have been greatly
> admired, as much by children, as by parents.[16]

Her reviews of all the Kilners' books are also extremely positive. A portion of the review of Life and Perambulations of a Mouse was given in Chapter II (p. 44). Of Jemima Placid she wrote, "These little volumes also justly claim a conspicuous place in the Infant Libraries." Mrs. Trimmer laments its limited distribution.[17] (These reviews may have also been influenced by her personal relationships with the authors. Letters of advice and friendship were passed between Mrs. Trimmer and Mrs. Barbauld, and the Kilners. No evidence up to this point has been found by this author indicating personal contact between the Edgeworth household and Mrs. Trimmer.)

Through the nineteenth century, commentary on the late

---

[16]Ibid., p. 302.

[17]Mrs. Trimmer, Guardian of Education, Vol. I (London: J. Hatchard, 1802), p. 124.

1700's didactic children's books continued to be printed--some-
times as criticism proper, other times within historical literary discussions. Many of the reviews found were positive.
The 1844 Quarterly Review article included in its listing of
important children's books Fabulous Histories, Evenings at
Home, and Maria Edgeworth stories. In the first full text on
children's literature, The Child and His Book (1882) by Mrs.
Field, lengthy and positive articles were written about Fabulous Histories, Evenings at Home and Maria Edgeworth's work
(see Chapter I, pp. 15-16). In Caroline Hewins' article in the
January 1888 issue of the Atlantic Monthly, she gave a brief
summary of the history of children's books. Although she did
not approve of heavy didactic overtones in children's literature, she chose Mrs. Barbauld and Maria Edgeworth to represent
the time period and devoted considerable space to them.[18] In
1896, Alexander Shand wrote in the Quarterly Review:

> The educational writers of the last quarter
> of the last century were more than talented. To
> the deliberate composition of unpretending works
> they brought a rare combination of qualities; and
> if the dead care for posthumous fame, they must
> have been rewarded beyond their utmost expecta-
> tions, for the books that were popular a hundred
> years ago are being reprinted and are selling
> largely . . . .[19]

> Evenings at Home was the forerunner of periodi-
> cals and journals which now cater indefatigably

[18]Caroline Hewins, "The History of Children's Books,"
Atlantic Monthly 61 (January 1888): 121-122.

[19]"Children Yesterday and Today," The Quarterly Review 183
(April 1896), reprinted in Lance Salway, ed., The Peculiar Gift
(Harmondsworth, Middlesex: Penguin Books, 1976), p. 77.

> for the tastes . . . of juveniles. 'The Trans-
> migrations of Indur' . . . . We know that it
> left ineffaceable impressions on the memory of
> veteran men of letters and genius . . . .[20]
>
> Mrs. Trimmer . . . originated the juvenile
> romance pure and simple . . . .[21]
>
> [of Miss Edgeworth] there is a wonderful fascina-
> tion in the stories, which had all the charm of a
> Protean introspection of the personages and of a
> novel and flowing style.[22]

It must be pointed out that the five selected books as

well as the whole of the didactic school were not always thought

of positively. As early as 1802, Charles Lamb was one of the

first who disapproved of this form of writing. In his oft

quoted letter to Coleridge, Lamb remarked:

> Mrs. Barbauld's stuff has banished all the old
> classics of the nursery . . . . Mrs. B's and
> Mrs. Trimmer's nonsense lay in piles about . . . .
> Science has succeeded to Poetry no less in the
> walks of children than with men. Is there no
> possibility of averting this sore evil? Think
> what you would have been now, if instead of being
> fed with Tales and old wives' fables in child-
> hood, you had been crammed with geography and
> natural history? Damn them!--I mean the cursed
> Barbauld Crew, those Blights and Blasts of all
> that is Human in man and child.[23]

In the later half of the nineteenth century, the Romantic

view of the child was strongly entrenched in child rearing and

educational theories. From this new conceptualization, the

---

[20]Ibid., p. 81.

[21]Ibid., p. 83.

[22]Ibid., p. 86.

[23]Introduction by J. H. Plumb, Early Children's Books and
Their Illustration--The Pierpont Morgan Library, by Gerald
Gottlieb (Boston: David R. Godine, 1975), pp. xi, xii.

fairy tales and fantasy of Anderson, Lear, Dodgson, etc.,
emerged. The older didactic style came under strong attack
from some reviewers. Yet this negative commentary was not
totally one sided. As Edward Salmon wrote in 1887, "the kind
of verse and prose supplied by Mesdames Barbauld and Trimmer
. . . though they may have many weak points, and are not exactly suited to the last quarter of the nineteenth century, I cannot understand Charles Lamb's overpowering objection to them."[24]

From the "eye witness accounts" of the children, nineteenth century adult recollections of childhood reading, contemporary and nineteenth century reviews, the researcher can
gain insight into how these forgotten children's books were received by their reading public. However, a much easier way to
assess contemporary popularity, and one that produces a greater
amount of documentation, is an investigation into the reprinting data of the specific books. Material found in these reprinting lists--number of editions published, number of publishing houses involved, life span (the actual number of years
the book was in print)--indicates marketability, thus popularity. This type of documentary evidence is reliable and
found without difficulty in The National Union Catalogue Pre-
1956 Imprints. It is very strange indeed that this data is
overlooked in contemporary criticisms of historical children's

---

[24]Edward Salmon, "Literature for the Little Ones," in
Juvenile Literature As It Is (London: Henry J. Drane, 1888),
reprinted in Lance Salway, ed., The Peculiar Gift (Harmondsworth, Middlesex: Penguin Books, 1976), p. 51.

books.[25] Without this type of information, a distorted view of
the books can occur. The rest of this chapter will be devoted
to the analysis of the reprintings of Fabulous Histories, The
Parent's Assistant, Evenings at Home, The Life and Perambulations of a Mouse, and Jemima Placid.

In analyzing this reprinting data, the following criteria
have been established to assess the popularity and success of
the five selected books:

(1) The life span of the books--indicating length of
popularity;

(2) Reprintings within the first years of publication--
indicating immediate response of the buying public;

(3) Geographical distribution of these books--indicating
that these books were selling beyond London and its immediate
environs (the city of initial publication);

(4) The number of publishing houses involved--indicating
marketability; and the number of reprintings per publishing
house--indicating the success of the firms' initial publication;[26]

(5) The illustrators/engravers commissioned--indicating
investment of capital;

(6) Special Comments--noteworthy and unique information

---

[25]Nothing is mentioned except for an occasional comment
referring to the long life spans of Fabulous Histories and The
Parent's Assistant.

[26]It should be noted that although a publishing house reprinted a book, the format may have been altered. Page numbers
and/or size varied, depending on the publisher's whim.

found in the reprinting data that is particularly pertinent. This may include noting of engraved plates, colored illustration, library series (i.e., a series of books published in similar bindings and format, under one name such as "Miniature Classics").

Summary and Classification of the Reprinting Data

The Parent's Assistant by Maria Edgeworth. 3 vols., 1796

1. Life Span

> 111 years (1796-1907). It should be noted that Sylvia
> Patterson reported that it was reprinted in the Water-
> gate Classics Series, 1948.[27] Also in the Graded List
> of Books for Children, compiled by Nora Beust in 1930,
> Maria Edgeworth's Tales, with "stories taken from 'The
> Parent's Assistant,'" was recommended reading for grades
> 4-6. Since the price of $2.50 is given, one can assume
> the book was currently in print.[28]

2. Reprinting Immediately After Initial Publication

> a. In the year of first publication, two editions were
> issued.
>
> b. Two years after the initial publication, it was re-
> printed in Dublin.
>
> c. By 1800 (four years after initial publication) the
> third edition was published.

3. Geographic Distribution

> London
> Dublin
> Boston
> New York
> Georgetown

---

[27]Sylvia Patterson, Rousseau's Emile, and Early Children's Literature (Metuchen, New Jersey: Scarecrow Press, 1971), p. 99.

[28]Nora Beust, Graded List of Books for Children (Chicago: American Library Association, 1930), p. 41.

Philadelphia
Paris
(Three countries, seven cities)

4. Publishing Houses (listed by city and in order of publishing date)

London

J. Johnson (5)*
R. Hunter (8)
G. Routledge, distributed also in New York (10)
Baldwin and Cradock (3)
Longman (3)
Hamilton and Co. (1)
Whittaker and Co. (1)
Houston and Co. (1)
W. Tegg (1)
Smith, Elder, and Co. (1)
Simpkin, Marshall and Co. (1)
Macmillan, distributed also in New York (3)

Philadelphia

W. P. Hazard (3)
J. B. Bradley (1)
Lippincott (3)

New York

W. L. Allison (1)
E. Duychinck (1)
W. Burgess (2)
Harper and Brothers (3)
Warne and Routledge (2)
J. Miller (2)
Hurd and Houghton (5)
Allen Brothers (1)
American Publishers Corp. (1)

Boston

Wells (1)
Monroe and Francis (4)
C. S. Francis (2)
Houghton, Mifflin (2)

Georgetown

Joseph Mulligan (1)

---

*number of times publishing houses reprinted the book

Paris

Baldry (2)
Stassin and Xavier (1)

5. Illustrators/Engravers

   A. Anderson
   Chris Hammond
   F. A. Frazer
   H. W. Herrick
   Phiz (pseudonym--Hablot Browne)

6. Special Comments

   a. Illustrations in color--4 editions.

   b. The 1870, London edition was published by nine pub-
       lishing houses.

   c. 44 reprints listed with frontispiece and/or il-
       lustrations.

   d. Published in two home library series--Allison's
       Select Library and Baudry's European Library.

   e. The 1822, London edition, published by R. Hunter,
       expanded into seven volumes. The seventh volume
       included "Little Plays for Children."

   f. Introduction in the Macmillan editions of 1897,
       1903, and 1907, by Anne T. Richie (noted biographer).

   g. Pseudonym of "M. E." was noted in the 1796 edition.

Summary and Classification of Reprinting Data

<u>Evenings at Home</u> by Mrs. Anna Barbauld and Dr. John Aiken.   6
vols., 1792-1796

1. Life Span

    108? years (1792-190?).

2. Reprintings Immediately After Initial Publication

    (The book was originally issued in six volumes, each

    volume printed as soon as it was written.)

    a. Published five times from 1792-1800.

    b. By 1795, three editions had been issued.

    c. From 1792-1800, it was published in four cities and

        two continents--London, Dublin, Salem and Phila-

        delphia.

3. Geographical Distribution

        London
        Dublin
        Salem
        Boston
        Cambridge
        Pittsburgh
        Philadelphia
        Halifax
        (2 countries, 1 British Colony, 8 cities)

4. Publishing Houses (listed by city and in order of publica-
                        tion date)
        <u>London</u>

        J. Johnson (9)*
        Baldwin, Cradock and Joy (5)
        Cornish (2)
        Longman (2)
        Scott (2)
        H. G. Bohn (4)
        Longman (2)
        Simkin, Marshall & Co. (1)

_____

    *number of times publishing houses reprinted the book

London (cont.)

Hamilton (1)
Nelson, also in New York (1)
H. Washbourne (1)
Routledge, also in New York (9)
Ward and Lock (1)
F. Warne and Co., also in New York (2)
Milner (1)

Salem

T. C. Cushing (2)

Dublin

Colbert (1)

Pittsburgh

C. H. Kay (2)

Philadelphia

T. Dobsen (2)
A. Bartram (1)
T. T. Ash (1)
Lippincott (2)
T. DeSilver (1)
Kay and Troutman (3)
Troutman and Hayes (1)

Halifax

Milner and Sowerby (2)

Boston

T. C. Cushing (2)
Cumming and Hilliard (1)
Hilliard and Metcalf (1)
D. Lothrop and Co. (1)
Houghton Mifflin (1)
Crosby and Nichols (2)

New York

Harper (and Brothers) (6)
T. Longworth (1)
A. T. Goodrich and Co. (1)
Orville A. Roorback (1)
C. S. Francis and Co. (3)
Cassell (2)

New York (cont.)

Hurd and Houghton (1)
Hurd (1)

5. Illustrators/Engravers

    A. Anderson
    Brothers Dalziel
    Engravings after Harvey and Chapman, by Adams

6. Special Comments

    a. Illustrations in color--3 editions.

    b. 33 reprints listed with frontispiece and/or
        illustrations.

    c. Published in two home library series--Bohn's Minia-
        ture Classics and Incident and Adventure Library.

    d. In the 189_, London edition, published by F. Warne,
        one title change noted.

    e. By 1853, the nineteenth edition had been reprinted.

    f. Revised four times.

Summary and Classification of the Reprinting Data

Fabulous Histories by Mrs. Trimmer.   1786

1. Life Span

     133 years (1786-1919).

2. Reprintings Immediately After Initial Publication

     a. Two editions were issued in the first year of
         publication.

     b. Five editions were issued within the first five
         years of publication.

     c. In the first year of printing, three publishing
         houses took up the books for sales.

     d. By 1794, it was published in three countries.

3. Geographical Distribution

     London
     Dublin
     Philadelphia
     New York
     Boston
     Frankfort-on-the-Main
     (4 countries, 6 cities)

4. Publishing Houses (listed by city and in order of publish-
                        ing date)

     London

     T. Longman (4)*
     G. G. J. and J. Robinson (4)
     J. Johnson (4)
     Griffith and Farran (6)
     Routledge--also in New York (3)
     Nelson--also in New York (1)
     Bell (1)
     Warne (2)

---

     *number of times publishing house reprinted the book

Dublin

W. Watson (1)
Society for Promoting the United and Scriptural Educa-
    tion of the Poor in Ireland (1)
S. McMullin (1)

Philadelphia

Wm. Gibbons (1)
Jacob Johnson (1)
A. Altemus (1)

Boston

D. C. Heath (2)
Monroe & Francis (2)

Frankfort

P. H. Guilhauman (1)

New York

E. P. Dutton (1)
Dodd & Mead (1)
Scribner, Welford (1)
C. S. Francis (3)
Blakeman & Mason (1)
Frederick Stokes (1)

5. Illustrators/Engravers

   Harrison Weir
   C. M. Howard
   Giacomelli
   Henry Roundtree

6. Special Comments

   a. Illustrations in color--1 edition.

   b. 22 reprints with illustrations and/or frontis-

      piece noted.

   c. Title changed noted six times.

   d. Four revised editions.

   e. Introduction to Heath edition by Edward Everett Hale

      (noted clergyman and author).

f. Published in two home library series--Francis and
    Co.'s Little Library, Warne's National Books.

g. Issued as a "gift" book--Landsdowne Gift Books.

Summary and Classification of the Reprinting Data

The Life and Perambulations of a Mouse by Dorothy Kilner. 1783?

1. Life Span

    69? years (178?-1849).

2. Reprintings Immediately After Initial Publication

    a. Two editions noted.

3. Geographical Distribution

    London
    Philadelphia
    (2 cities)

4. Publishing Houses (listed by city and in order of publish-
                        ing date)
    London

    John Marshall (2)*
    Baldwin, Cradock and Joy (1)
    Harris (1)

    Philadelphia

    Appleton (2)

5. Illustrators/Engravers

    William Croome

6. Special Comments

    a. Illustration in color--2 editions (out of seven

        editions).

    b. Six reprints listed with frontispiece and/or

        illustrations.

    c. First edition listed, bound in Dutch gilt paper.

    d. Pseudonyms of "M. P." or "by a lady" used throughout

        listings.

---

*number of times publishing house reprinted the book

e. In 1800 London edition, bound with Newbery's

Primrose Pretty Face.

Summary and Classification of the Reprinting Data

Jemima Placid by Mary Jane Kilner. 1785?

1. Life Span

    34? years (1785?-1819).

2. Reprintings Immediately After Initial Publication

    Three editions were published in the late 1780's.

3. Geographical Distribution

    London

4. Publishing Houses (listed by city in order of publishing
                              date)
    London

    John Marshall (2)*
    Baldwin, Cradock and Joy (1)

5. Special Comments

    a. No author is listed. The National Union Catalogue
        incorrectly attributes this book to Dorothy Kilner.

    b. Three editions (out of 4 reprintings listed) listed
        with illustrations and/or frontispiece.

    c. Early publications bound in Dutch gilt paper.

    d. 178? London edition published by John Marshall
        issued in two separate printings--one in gilt paper,
        and a more expensive volume bound in red (leather?).

---

*number of times publishing house reprinted the book

Analysis and Conclusions

As seen in the summary and classification of the reprinting data, the evidence strongly indicates that Fabulous Histories, Evenings at Home, and The Parent's Assistant were extremely popular books and considered highly marketable by publishers over a long period of time. Although Life and Perambulations of a Mouse and Jemima Placid had much shorter life
spans and more limited distributions, they did go through a
number of reprintings with the early inclusion of illustrations
and fancy bindings. This indicates that they too were successful in their day. The five books collectively went through 193
reprintings. Sixty-eight publishing houses were involved with
the five selected books. The Routledge firm, one of the leading publishers of children's books in the Victorian era, reprinted in all, 22 editions of Fabulous Histories, Evenings at
Home, and The Parent's Assistant. The books were included in
seven home library series and one gift book series. The geographical distribution of publication spread over two continents, five countries, one British colony, and twelve cities.

This information along with the other documentary evidence
of actual children's responses and nineteenth century adult
recollections disproves J. H. Plumb's suggestion that these
books possibly were not read by children.[29] This evidence also
strongly questions the accuracy of many of the twentieth

---

[29] J. H. Plumb, introduction to Early Children's Books and
Their Illustration--The Pierpont-Morgan Library, by Gerald
Gottlieb (Boston: David R. Godine, 1975), p. xxii.

century negative comments about these books (see Chapter I, pp. 8-11). If these didactic books contain, as suggested, such poor writing, weak characterization, inappropriate themes, etc., then what accounts for their success? It is true that these five didactic children's books, in comparison to modern children's literature, are outmoded in theme and style. This should not negate their historical importance as well as the esteem held for them in the late eighteenth and nineteenth centuries. When modern literary historians ignore documentary evidence, as just given, their resulting conclusions are distorted, and at times inaccurate.

The data from the reprinting lists gives ample evidence indicating popularity and marketability of the five selected books. However, a further investigation should be made to ascertain what factors (other than literary merit which will be discussed in the next chapter) may have contributed to the large number of reprintings and the many publishing houses involved. A study of related research has suggested six circumstances which may have contributed to these large numbers: 1) contractual agreements between author and publisher, 2) lack of an international copyright law, 3) use of illustrations in the books, 4) the growing belief in the power of the printed page, 5) the contemporary child rearing practice (and conceptualization of childhood) that prohibited the young from reading adult literature, and 6) the rising rate of literacy in eighteenth century England. These aforementioned conditions do not undermine the indicated popularity of the books themselves, nor do they diminish the reliability of the findings from the National Union Catalogue. Rather, they give insight into the growing phenomenon of children's literature in the eighteenth and nineteenth centuries. Also this added information further indicates that the five selected books did indeed fulfill society's and publishers' requirements for successful children's literature in this time period.

In the eighteenth and nineteenth centuries, circumstances were such that an author did not have to exclusively sign with one publishing firm. Unless a book was specifically commissioned by a publishing house (e.g., Marshall's commissioning children's books from the Kilners, or John Newbery engaging Oliver Goldsmith and Richard Johnson to write for him), the authors had more freedom than today, in signing with multiple firms. For example, the 1822 London edition of The Parent's Assistant was printed for three firms simultaneously. The estate of Mrs. Trimmer contracted with three different firms in publishing The Life and Writings of Mrs. Trimmer in 1814. This contractual situation, in part explains the incredibly large number of publishing houses involved with the books. However, these multiple publishing houses would not have agreed to the contract, if they were not reasonably certain that the books would sell in large numbers.

Another factor which explains the many firms involved, is that in the eighteenth and most of the nineteenth centuries, an international copyright law did not exist. The result of this was that any American firm could produce and sell any British

book without paying royalties. Book piracy, on both sides of
the Atlantic, was rampant up to the mid-nineteenth century.
One of the earliest and most notorious of these pirates was
Isaiah Thomas of Boston who stole much of the juvenile library
published by John Newbery, with substantial financial gain.[30]
In the first half of the nineteenth century, there were American attempts to pass such a law, but without any success. In
1837, Henry Clay was one of the first who forcefully proposed
such a law. He failed in his endeavors; so did further attempts made by others in 1840, 1884, and 1885.[31] It was not
until 1891 that the International Copyright Law was passed,
finally ending over 120 years of piracy.[32] All American firms
reprinting any of the five selected British children's books,
up to this date, could do so incurring no additional expenses
except for printing and bindings. Piracy or not, these selected books would not have been picked up by American firms
unless they were considered financially sound. It should also
be noted that many highly respected publishing firms were selling these books. If a prominent house was reprinting the book
it would seem to be a safe investment for a smaller or newer
firm to also duplicate it. Also, prominent firms would not
risk their reputation by continuing to reprint books not

---

[30] In England, George Putnam published without permission
382 American books between 1841 and 1846. Charles Madison,
Book Publishing in America (New York: McGraw Hill, 1968), p. 16.

[31] Ibid., p. 59.

[32] Alec Ellis, How to Find Out About Children's Books
(Oxford: Pergamon Press, 1966), p. 10.

respected by literary critics and the public.

The following is an alphabetical listing of the most prominent publishers who reprinted one or more of the five selected books.

Appleton: A firm ranked in 1865 as the second largest publishing house in America. Mr. Appleton was considered a "first rate business man."[33] His firm was known for its many school texts, notably Webster's Elementary Spelling Book, encyclopedias, medical books, and the publishing of Commodore Perry's and Thomas Hart Benton's writings.

Baldwin, Cradock and Joy: One of the early British publishers of children's books. It also sold the popular London Magazine.

Cummings and Hilliard: A Boston firm begun in 1813, publishing the writings of the early American patriots and the reprintings of popular English authors. In 1837, they were bought out by Charles C. Little and James Brown, thus forming the initial backbone of the successful publishing house of Little, Brown, and Co.

E. P. Dutton: A well respected American house, which remained prominent well into the twentieth century. The firm was known for its many school and religious books. Mr. Dutton was one of the first Americans to establish business relations with a British publishing

---

[33]Madison, Book Publishing in America, p. 72.

house.

Harper (and Brothers): This American company emerged as one of
the largest publishers in the world. In 1853, it
was publishing 1,549 books in 2,028 volumes. The
Harper Brothers were pioneers in printing inexpensive, popular books.

Heath: Begun in a partnership with Ginn in 1878, the firm
originally specialized in children's classics and
scholarly journals. In 1885, Heath established his
own firm and by 1900 was ranked third in American
sales of textbooks. He was involved in school cur-
riculum and maintained that it was publishers who
were largely responsible for innovations and improvements in educational methodologies.

Houghton-Mifflin: Mr. Houghton in his day was referred to as
"par excellence, the American printer."[34] The firm
was particularly well known for their Riverside Literature Series which became a classic in the schools.

Joseph Johnson: A highly respected eighteenth century publisher who sold the writings of Priestly, John New-
ton, and Erasmus Darwin along with children's books.
He was considered "a man of honor and integrity" by
his authors.[35] A strong believer in the freedom of
the press, Mr. Johnson was imprisoned for nine

---

[34] Ibid., p. 140.

[35] Frank A. Mumby, Publishing and Bookselling (London:
Jonathan Cape, 1956), p. 200.

months for publishing the prohibited work of Gilbert and Wakefield.

Lippincott: This Philadelphia based firm was originally begun in 1850, and today is still a well respected publishing house. Mr. Lippincott was immediately successful and in 1853 the total sales of the firm came close to two million dollars. He was well known for his reference books and dictionaries, and established a London office.

John Marshall: This was one of the early children's publishing houses, specializing in didactic literature. Mr. Marshall prided himself in divesting from his children's books "that prejudicial nonsense and Tales of Hobgoblins, Witches, Fairies, Love, Gallentry, etc."[36] He actively solicited writing from the Kilners.[37] He was also responsible for publishing the enormously successful Cheap Repository Tracts.

Macmillan: A very prominent British house which published leading authors, and the successful Macmillan Magazine. A New York office was opened and today is still a leader in publishing.

Rivington: This was an early British firm begun in 1711 on the famous "Paternoster Row" which later was the address

---

[36] Janet Adam Smith, Children's Illustrated Books (London: Collins, 1958), p. 13.

[37] Percy Muir, English Children's Books from 1600-1900 (New York: Frederick A. Praeger, 1954), p. 9.

of many important publishing houses. It was the
leading theological publisher in eighteenth century
England.

Routledge: A prominent publisher of fine Victorian children's
books, this firm issued the works of Kate Greenaway
and Randolph Caldecott. The Dalziel Brothers engraved many of the Routledge books, and it was this
firm that popularized the "toy-books" of the late
nineteenth century.

The one important eighteenth century publishing firm most
noticeably missing from this list is John Newbery's. Mr. Newbery could not have published any of the five selected books,
since he died in 1768, before any of these books were written.
His immediate successors were Carnan and F. Newbery, with Elizabeth Newbery taking over shortly thereafter. During this time
period (1768-1802) it should be noted that the Newbery firm
used Mrs. Trimmer's name for its publication of Ladder to
Learning, the First Step (1780).[38] The firm also issued Juvenile Rambles through the Paths of Nature deliberately rewritten
by Richard Johnson from Mrs. Trimmer's Introduction to the
Knowledge of Nature.[39] In 1799, Elizabeth Newbery sold The
Silver Thimble, "by Mrs. Trimmer." It is highly doubtful that
Mrs. Trimmer authored this text or the 1780 book, but it does

---

[38]S. Roscoe, John Newbery and His Successors: A Bibliography (Wormley, Hertfordshire: Five Owls Press, 1973), p. 259.

[39]Peter Opie, "John Newbery and His Successors," Book Collector 24 (Summer, 1975): 265.

strongly demonstrate the renown and marketability of the Trimmer name.[40] Elizabeth Newbery sold the firm to her general
manager, John Harris, in 1802. He published The Life and Perambulations of a Mouse in 1828. In 1756, Griffith and Farran
took over the firm and reprinted Fabulous Histories six times.

Illustrations make a book more attractive, thus may increase sales. When artists/engravers of some prominence are
commissioned, marketability is further increased. The illustrated editions of the five selected books, especially those
done by such well known illustrators/engravers as Anderson, the
Dalziel Brothers, Weir, et al., may have accounted for the many
reprintings. However, the inclusion of illustrations also indicates popularity of a book, since it involves a capital investment on the part of the publisher. The money would not
have originally been laid out if financial gain was not expected. This becomes even more true when artists of prominence
were commissioned or when the illustrations were colored.
Respected illustrators in the mid 1800's received up to 15
pounds and 15 shillings per plate.[41] Engravers would then have
to be paid to prepare the illustration for publication. It was
well worth the publisher's while to hire a good one, since it
was the engraver who chose the method and medium for reproduc-
tion. Depending on his talents, an engraver could ruin the
best of illustrations or develop the printed form far better

---

[40]S. Roscoe, John Newbery and His Successors, p. 262.

[41]Percy Muir, Victorian Illustrated Books (New York:
Praeger, 1971), p. 27.

than the original.[42] Adding color also incurred costs. Not
only did the colorists have to be paid, but the process was
time consuming, delaying the actual sale of the books. Hand
coloring was accomplished by a squad of children seated around
a table. One color was allotted to each child, and following
the model, the child then placed his color on the appropriate
section(s), page after page.[43]

Below is an alphabetical list of the more prominent illus-
trators/engravers involved with one or more of the five selected books:

J. A. Adams: One of the best American engravers of the mid
            nineteenth century. A contemporary ranked him
            "worthy . . . beside the best of the great old
            timers in England."[44] His most important illustra-
            tions were found in the Harper's Illustrated Bible
            (1846). This was outstanding not only for its tech-
            nical innovations but it also was the most exten-
            sively illustrated book in America, in its time.
            Over 1,600 illustrated vignettes and borders were
            included in this text.

Alexander Anderson: An apprentice to the famous Thomas Bewick,
            Mr. Anderson is called "the father of wood engraving

---

[42]Philip James, English Book Illustration: 1800-1900 (New
York: Penguin Books, 1947), p. 7.

[43]Smith, Children's Illustrated Books, pp. 15-16.

[44]Muir, Victorian Illustrated Books, p. 251.

in America."[45] He worked for many printers from New Haven to Charlestown, and remained prominent in his profession throughout the first half of the nine-teenth century.

William Croome: An important American illustrator and engraver in the nineteenth century who is best known as the illustrator of the famous Peter Parley series, first published by S. Goodrich in 1827. He also did the engravings for Γ. O. Darley, America's best known early illustrator.

The Dalziel Brothers: These two men were the greatest wood en-gravers of the nineteenth century. They engraved Tenniel's illustrations for Alice in Wonderland and Arabian Nights. They were also responsible for re-producing for printing the works of Whistler and A. Hughes. Their skill was supreme in capturing the style of each of the artists with whom they worked.

Chris Hammond: A respected British artist who worked for many of the prominent publishing houses in the nineteenth century.

Phiz (pseud.): Hablot Browne. Some of Mr. Browne's work is considered the best of Victorian illustration. He leapt into fame with his first commission at 24, and for the next 30 years he was one of the most sought

[45]Bertha Mahoney, Louise Latimer, and Beulah Folmsbee, eds., Illustrators of Children's Books: 1744-1945 (Boston: The Horn Book, 1961), p. 89.

after illustrators in London. He is best known for

his marvelous depictions of Dickens' characters. He

also did many illustrations for children's books.

Harrison Weir: A well respected British illustrator whose work

was found in the McGuffey Readers, beginning reading

books of one syllable, and animal stories. He was

one of the first artists who wrote his own chil-

dren's stories as well as illustrating them.

It should be noted that the Kilners' books were illustrated before 1800. Children's book illustration was not common in the 1700's, despite Mr. Newbery's noteworthy attempts in
this area. Gleason White wrote in 1897 that a text on children's illustrated books "could scarce have been compiled a
century ago for there was practically no material for it."[46]
It was not until the mid nineteenth century that book illustration began to flourish.[47]

There also seemed to be a growing belief in the late
eighteenth century, in the power of the printed page, which may
have influenced the need for children's books, thus the many
reprintings. We of the twentieth century tend to be more cyni-
cal in our response to the printed word. We question the
sources used, the intent of the author. We question if a book

_____

[46]Gleason White, Children's Books and Their Illustrators,
Monograph of The Studio (Special Winter Number, 1897-1898), p.
7.

[47]Michael Angelo Titmarsh [pseud., William Thackery], "On
Some Illustrated Books," Fraser's Magazine (April, 1846): 496.

will have a grave and long lasting impact upon the reader. We read for enjoyment, to learn something, to perhaps even gain insights, but we generally do not expect profound changes in thought or personality. This was not the case in the late 1700's. It seems there was a general agreement that reading could indeed seriously affect the reader--especially the young and the lower classes. Material was specifically written for the poor to instill proper deportment and thinking, and to quell any class jealousies. Hannah More's Cheap Repository Tracts and Mrs. Trimmer's The Story of the Donkey were created especially for this purpose. Likewise, literature, for the young was also carefully monitored to insure that suitable reading material was given to the young. This monitoring, or censorship if you will, is seen throughout The Guardian of Education. A sense of urgency seems to emanate from many of the reviews prompting parents to immediately cut out or blacken objectionable pages or selections before the child saw them. Mrs. Trimmer is most meticulous in her instructions, describing exact page numbers and even specific lines.

Reading material for the young gained a new importance in the 1700's. Children's books became the "symbol of government of children." Child rearing manuals urged that children should be kept at their books.[48] This importance of the children's book was demonstrated in a letter written by Mr. James Murray in the second half of the eighteenth century. Forced to flee

_____

[48]Lloyd de Mause, ed., The History of Childhood (New York: Psychohistory Press, 1974), p. 365.

Boston because of his Loyalist activities, Mr. Murray requested
the following items needed for his new home: "Everlasting 4
yards; batting 1 piece; of gingham two gown patterns; . . .
Locke on Education,--five children's books."[49] It is quite re-
markable that in a time of obvious stress and estrangement, the
exiled Mr. Murray requested along with the practical necessi-
ties of life, children's books. An American mother was over-
heard saying in 1801, "We all wish that our young folks should
love reading; and the fondness for books is a mark of sense,
and may be conducive to improvement."[50] In the preface of
Davy's New Hat (1817), the author Robert Bloomfield wrote:
"The longer I live the more I am convinced of the importance of
children's books."[51]

Locke's conceptualization of the child as a Tabula Rasa
also fostered this new belief in the power of the children's
book. Since the young mind was seen as a blank sheet of paper,
the child was believed to be extremely vulnerable to all incom-
ing information. Therefore the printed page given to the child
had to be of the most upstanding quality, in order to fill his
mind with the proper impressions. For the first time since the
Middle Ages, children were deliberately shielded from adult

---

[49] Halsey, Forgotten Books of the American Nursery, p. 99.

[50] Monica Kiefer, American Children through Their Books:
1700-1835 (Philadelphia: University of Pennsylvania Press,
1948), p. 91.

[51] Charles Welsh, "Some Notes on the History of Books for
Children, 1800-1850," Newbery House Magazine (August 1890):
85.

reading material. In the previous centuries, children took much of the adult literature as their own. The tales of King Arthur and Robin Hood in the Medieval centuries, Pilgrim's Progress in the 1600's, and Gulliver's Travels and Robinson Crusoe in the early 1700's were read and listened to as much by children as by adults. By the end of the eighteenth century, the literature intended for adults no longer was considered appropriate for the young.[52] True, some of the contemporary adult novels were a bit raucous and earthy for the young child, but a surprising number of these novels were as didactic in nature as the children's books.

What accounts for this concern? Perhaps parents felt that the inclusion of major characters rising from a lower station of life to a higher one (such as some of Richardson's heroines) might create within the child a feeling for class equality--an attitude not appropriate for the late eighteenth century.[53] This hypothesis, however, does not give a complete answer,

---

[52]This is not to say that children before this time period did not have their own literature, or that parental censorship over their readings did not exist. As early as 1554, Hugh Rodes in the Book of Nurture urged parents to "use them to read in the Bible, and other Godly books, but especially keep them from reading feigned fables, vain fantasies, wanton stories, and songs of love, which bring much mischief to youth." F. J. Harvey Darton, Children's Books in England: Five Centuries of Social Life (Cambridge: Cambridge University Press, 1958), p. 45. In the seventeenth century, the Puritans were particularly active in writing children's books, and were deeply concerned over their children's moral welfare. However, in the late eighteenth century a successful and strict separation of adult and children's literature occurred.

[53]F. E. Halliday, An Illustrated Cultural History of England (New York: Viking Press, 1967), p. 200.

since Miss Margery of the beloved <u>Goody Two Shoes</u> was quite poor and had the good fortune of marrying into the landed gentry. The real issue in this censorship may lie in Mrs. West's "Remarks on the Novels." "I would advise you to devote your literary hours to the perusal either of such works as communicate solid information, or such as abound in the playfulness of innocent humour. Those authors who powerfully excite our feelings are unsafe."[54] This comment was made to adults in the late eighteenth/early nineteenth century, but would be even more pertinent in regarding the reading of the impressionable young. Here again, the belief in the power of print is apparent. A novel is fiction, yet it is realistic in style. If an author wrote with clarity, a reader may become involved to such a degree in the story as to model the passions, jealousies and behaviors of the characters. "Passions' Angry Storms" were simply not acceptable in this time period.

It is hard to believe, however, that there was never a naughty late eighteenth century child who snuck into his parents' library to read forbidden books. The child may have been disappointed in the fare he found. With the exception of Smollett and Fielding, much of the adult literature of this era did not have the excitement and intrigue of such earlier classics as <u>Robinson Crusoe</u>. And the heroes and heroines of their own children's books, Lazy Lawrence, Rosamond, Simple Susan, et al., may have been more appealing to the young child than

---

[54]Trimmer, <u>The Guardian of Education</u>, Vol. I, pp. 77-78.

Pamela, Clarissa and other characters popular in adult novels.
Thus, the child's book had risen in esteem in the eyes of the
adult and may also have held an even greater role in juvenile
pleasure reading than ever before. These attitudes may well
have contributed to the many reprintings of the children's
books. At the same time, parents and publishers were being extremely selective in their choice of children's books to purchase and publish.

The literacy rate in eighteenth century England was rising, and this also may have contributed to the many reprintings. Brought on by the needs of the pre-industrial and agricultural revolutions and the new humanitarian attitude, educational opportunities spread for both the middle and lower
classes. This rise in literacy was most dramatically seen
among the new merchants and shopkeepers. This newly made reading audience was so hungry for the written page that it was the
custom to tear freshly published best sellers into a dozen
parts because no one could await their turn to read it.[55] The
numbers of readers in the lower classes was also increasing.
Robert Raikes estimated that by 1787, a quarter of a million
poor children were being taught to read in the Sunday
schools.[56] John Wesley pushed for literacy among his flock
saying, "Reading Christians are knowing Christians."[57] He

---

[55]Agnes Repplier, A Happy Half Century and Other Essays
(Boston: Houghton Mifflin, 1908), p. 13.

[56]Mary Thwaite, From Primer to Pleasure in Reading (Boston: The Horn Book, 1963), p. 59.

[57]Richard Altick, The English Common Reader: A Social

established reading rooms around England, and personally re-
wrote some of the classics in easier language.[58] This rising
literacy rate had a strong influence on book production in the
eighteenth century, which went beyond the large numbers of
books needed to satisfy the reading public. The writing style
actually changed because of it. The ornate, embellished writing of the 1600's and early 1700's became plainer, with a more
simplified vocabulary.[59]

Therefore, the increase in the actual numbers of readers,
the growing belief in the power of print, and the strong desire
on the part of adults to purchase suitable juvenile books, created a new and large market for children's literature. This
demand encouraged publishing houses to invest more and more
into this new literary genre. The contractual agreements of
the eighteenth and nineteenth centuries, and the lack of an
international copyright law also helped in fulfilling the public demand for more children's literature. Illustrated books,
particularly by eminent artists/engravers increased sales. All
of these factors and conditions help to explain why there were
so many publishing houses involved with the five selected books
and why there were so many reprintings. More importantly, this
information also strongly suggests that Fabulous Histories,

History of the Mass Reading Public--1800-1900 (Chicago: University of Chicago Press, 1957), p. 35.

[58]Ibid., p. 36.

[59]J. H. Plumb, England in the Eighteenth Century: 1714-
1815 (Harmondsworth, Middlesex: Penguin, 1950), p. 32.

Evenings at Home, The Parent's Assistant, The Life and Perambulations of a Mouse, and Jemima Placid were considered successful and proper children's literature by the publishers and the
public at large. Not only did these books fulfill the requirements of good children's literature for the society for which
they were originally intended, but also for many subsequent
generations.

CHAPTER IV

A CRITICAL ANALYSIS OF THE FIVE SELECTED
LATE EIGHTEENTH CENTURY BRITISH
DIDACTIC CHILDREN'S BOOKS

Introduction

Before beginning the critical analyses of the five selected didactic British children's books, it is important to
review definitions of children's literature. From these definitions, insights can be gained into the conceptual framework
traditionally used by commentators and critics in evaluation.
Arriving at a definition is no easy task. Children's literature is a unique art form. It is the only medium which is produced by one distinct group in a society or culture, the adults,
for another, the children. Jackson Pollack, Philip Roth,
Charles Ives create for their fellow adults. True, artists
primarily create for themselves, but there is also a kinship,
so to speak, between themselves and their intended audience.
This is not the case in children's literature. Ever since it
was decided that indeed children are a separate "specie," authors of children's books have been painfully aware that there
are specific differences between themselves and their young
readers. No matter how sincere the adult intentions, "children
and grown people frequently differ as to what is interesting to

children."[1] This difference between adult and child, this
"essence of childhood" is what authors try to capture in their
books for children. It is what makes writing for children so
particularly difficult, and perhaps it is this which also
causes the difficulty in arriving at a generally agreed upon
definition. Some critics have thrown up their hands in dismay
at the perplexity of the problem and responded that "there is
no definition for children's books":[2] "it is the magic that
eludes definition."[3]

For others, the purpose of children's literature is primarily seen as giving enjoyment to its audience. F. J. Harvey
Darton defines children's books as "works ostensibly to give
children spontaneous pleasure, and not to primarily teach them,
nor solely make them good, nor to keep them profitably quiet."[4]
Other commentators place greater emphasis on the educational
component in children's books. True children's literature is
seen by some as "literature marketed to children designed for
their amusement as well as for their edification,"[5] aiding in

---

[1]Clara Hunt, What Shall We Read to the Children? (Boston:
Houghton Mifflin, 1915), p. 5.

[2]Montrose Moses, Children's Books and Reading (New York:
Kennerly, 1907), p. 6.

[3]Lillian Smith, The Unreluctant Years (New York: Viking,
1953), p. 11.

[4]F. J. Harvey Darton, Children's Books in England: Five
Centuries of Social Life (Cambridge: Cambridge University
Press, 1958), p. 1.

[5]Francelia Butler, ed., Children's Literature, Vol. 10
(New Haven: Yale University, 1981), p. 1.

"his growth as an individual."[6] The definition is further expanded by others to incorporate the child's own internal responses. It should be literature "accessible to children,"[7] "that draws upon the emotional and intellectual experiences of children."[8] A fourth component included in some definitions is the one which looks at children's literature as art of the highest quality. As early as 1844, it was written, "The real secret of a children's book consists not merely in its being less dry and less difficult, but more rich in interest--more true to nature--more exquisite in art."[9] Approximately eighty years later Walter de la Mare reiterated "only the rarest kind of best in anything can be good enough for the young."[10] In Books, Children and Men, Paul Hazard wrote, "I like books that remain faithful to the very essence of art; namely those that offer to children an intuitive and direct way of knowledge, a simple beauty capable of being perceived immediately, arising in their souls a vibration which will endure all their lives."[11]

[6]Evelyn Robinson, Readings About Children's Literature (New York: David McKay, 1966), p. 77.

[7]Barbara Harrison, "Why Study Children's Literature?" The Quarterly Journal of the Library of Congress 38 (Fall 1981): 243.

[8]Blanche E. Weekes, Literature and the Child (New York: Silver Burdett Company, 1935), p. 4.

[9]Quarterly Review 71 (1844), p. 16.

[10]Sheila Egoff, G. T. Stubbs, L. F. Ashley, eds., Only Connect: Readings on Children's Literature (New York: Oxford University, 1969), p. 443.

[11]Paul Hazard, Books, Children and Men (Boston: The Horn Book, 1947), p. 42.

These descriptions list the major characteristics found in children's books. Certainly we wish the literature given to the young to be enjoyable, to allow them insights into themselves and the world they live in, to be readily identifiable with the young reader's interests, and to be of a high quality, "the best, the really excellent."[12] But these definitions are limiting in some respects. One aspect which is missed is that in truth, children's literature is as much written for the adult as it is for the child; for the adult is the purchaser and the major critic. Before the finished product ever reaches the child readers, it is scrutinized, analyzed, and surveyed by an adult audience. Almost all art forms have their mediators or middlemen, who stand between the artist and the public deciding what will be selected and accepted. But with children's books, these mediators are far more numerous and in a more powerful position. It is their voices--the publisher, the critic, the librarian, the parent--not the children's which is heard the loudest.[13] "The child himself hardly enters into the process . . . ."[14] For a children's book to be successful it must be acceptable to both adults and children.

This adult component is extremely important. It is the adults that demand high literary quality. More importantly,

---

[12]Harrison, "Why Study Children's Literature?" The Quarterly Journal of the Library of Congress 38 (Fall, 1981): 243.

[13]Peter Dickenson, "The Day of the Rabbit," The Quarterly Journal of the Library of Congress 38 (Fall, 1981): 218.

[14]Egoff, Only Connect, p. 36.

most adult critics and purchasers will not readily accept a
book that is not in accord with their society's goals for its
young. (Needless to say, the adults may not be in agreement
upon these goals.) Adults wish their children to become contented and productive members of society. Educational philosophies revolve around these goals; children's books, a natural
part of the child's education, also reflect this. Acceptable
themes and characters presented in children's literature depict
and demonstrate how the child can be useful and successful in
the society, and how to promote the society's welfare. In
Gillian Avery's studies into nineteenth century children's literature, she repeatedly found that the heroes and heroines reflect the best of what society desired for their young, in
terms of character and moral behavior. She strongly contends
that characters in children's books act as socializing agents.

Yet this function of children's literature as a socializing agent is often overlooked. One direct reference to this is
in the article, "Kids, Pull Up Your Socks." The author, Margot
Hentoff, writes that children's books have been one of the traditional methods used to teach adult values; the books act as a
bridge for the children to cross over to the adult side. To
omit this purpose seems odd to say the least. It does not at
all seem out of keeping for a society to create and present
literature to their young to teach both the expected mores and
society's ideals, dreams, and goals. Histories of children's
literature repeatedly stress the importance of, and joy received from the oral tradition of legends and myths. They

contend that these are the heart and core of children's literature. If legends are defined as the societal presentation of
its ideals, with heroes embodying the best qualities of the
culture, then we should not be surprised that children's stories continue to present to the young reader, characters who
teach the best ideas of that society.

What helps to determine society's goals for its children
is the current conceptualization of childhood and the related
child rearing practices. There is an extremely close relationship between children's literature and the conceptualization of
childhood. Children's books are written by adults, whose view
of the "essence of childhood" is determined by how that particular society and time period understands the nature of the
child. When reviewing children's books, especially historical
literature, it is important to remember that what the child is
thought to enjoy, what he is expected to learn, and how he
should act are determined by current philosophical beliefs.
When the critic takes as a definition that the purpose of children's books is to "ostensibly . . . give pleasure," he cannot
assume that the pleasure of the eighteenth century child is
identical to the twentieth century child's. If it is agreed
upon that children's books should aid in the "growth of the individual," the reviewer should not be so naive as to assume
that this conceptualization of human growth and potential is
identical through the ages. Tom Wolfe's description of the "Me
Generation" of the 1970's with its individualistic striving for
personal growth independent of social considerations, is as far

a cry from the notion of individual growth in the early nineteenth century as it was from the 1950's. When trying to understand what children's literature is, there must be the
underlying assumption that the children's book is a distinct
product of its time period, reflecting the contemporary conceptualization of childhood and its accompanying child rearing
practices.

Another aspect of the traditional definitions which limits
the scope and nature of children's literature is the expecta-
tion that it should be "a jewel of great price."[15] Certainly
the finest literary quality should be striven for, but the
genius needed to create such a work is unique. A Charles Dodgson or a Kenneth Grahame is as rare as a James Joyce. To always demand this level of excellence is unrealistic and impossible. If, as Lillian Smith suggests, "We should instinctively
reject the mediocre, the unrewarding,"[16] a whole body of literature is lost. The Bobbsey twins, the Hardy boys, and the
other assorted Dicks and Janes will never be considered classic
children's literature, but they are read avidly by the young.
Their intrinsic worth lies in the facts that they are enjoyed
by children, and that children do learn something from them.[17]

_____

[15]Alice Dalgliesh, First Experiences with Literature (New
York: Charles Scribner's Sons, 1932), p. ix.

[16]Smith, The Unreluctant Years, p. 13.

[17]Deep philosophical or psychological insights may not be
gained from such books, but if nothing more the children learn
the very important concept that enjoyment can be received from
the written page.

To make such a statement as that of Miss Smith seems terribly unfair. We adults do not always reach for a Willa Cather or a Hemingway in our leisure reading. Certainly this is attested to by the volumes and volumes of romances and detective novels sold. Should not our children be allowed the same luxury of choice?[18]

Perhaps then children's literature should be defined as literature enjoyed by the young, which aids in the transmission of society's expectations, ideals, and goals. The first part of the definition includes the aspects that the books should be well written, and directly related to the child's interests, curiosity and sense of wonder. These make the books appealing to read. The second part is inherently connected to the conceptualization of childhood and related theories, for they define the goals for the society's younger members. When the insights into the human character are universal, when the ideals and goals presented embody the most heroic of mankind, when the style is truly superlative, then the book transcends the time period in which it was written, and becomes a classic.

Although a comprehensive definition of children's literature may be difficult to articulate, the criteria of what makes good children's literature are generally agreed upon. Not only are the modern critics in accord, these standards have remained

---

[18]The reading of the second rate (as one might call the less than classics) proves that children somehow manage to have a say in their choice of literature. Their criterion, suggests M. Moses, is a simple one: The material is enjoyable. Montrose Moses, "Convalescent Children's Literature," North American Review 221 (April 1925): 528.

relatively unchanged in the last one hundred and forty years. In the 1844 article in the _Quarterly Review_, considered a milestone in early children's literature criticism,[19] the qualities ascribed to or prescribed for good children's books are the same as those used by modern reviewers. The anonymous author[20] wrote an essay on what children's literature should be, and then gave examples of good children's books in an annotated list. Below are listed a summary of her criteria along with supportive comments made by modern reviewers.

(1) The 1844 author advises not to write down to children.[21] Condescension is oppressive[22] and transparent. As the Newbery Award winning author Henrich Van Loon reiterated, "A good writer for children has something to say; he says it in the best way possible and trusts the child will understand . . . ."[23]

(2) The story should not over explain, for "regular series of lessons never do so much good as when a gap is left here and

---

[19]Virginia Haviland, ed., _Children's Literature: Views and Reviews_ (New York: Lothrop, Lee and Shepard, 1973), p. 8.

[20]Thwaite identifies the author as Elizabeth Rigby. Mary Thwaite, _From Primer to Pleasure in Reading_ (Boston: The Horn Book, 1963), p. 104. The _Pooles Index_ also cites Miss Rigby as the author. However Welsh refers to her as Lady Eastlake. Charles Welsh, "The Children's Books that Have Lived," _The Library_ NSI 1900: 321.

[21]_Quarterly Review_, 1844, p. 3.

[22]Anne Carroll Moore, _My Roads to Childhood: Views and Reviews of Children's Books_ (Boston: Horn Book, 1961), p. 25.

[23]Smith, _The Unreluctant Years_, p. 13.

there for the mind's own operations."[24] Katherine Paterson

wrote in 1981, "what is left out of a work of art is as impor-

tant as, if not more important than, what is put in."[25]

(3) Let the style of a child's book be such that it does

not preach. This not only weakens the story and makes it less

enjoyable but also belittles the child "through the pertinacity

of admonition, injunction, and advice."[26] The 1844 author was

not implying that moral teaching is inappropriate in literature

for the young, just that it should be treated gently and grow

naturally out of the story. In a similar vein, Hillaire Belloc

wrote in the early part of this century, "the sense of justice

. . . is especially the clearest thing in a child's creed . . .

one may fearlessly adventure into plain moral teaching of all

kinds and please an audience of children immensely thereby, so

long as the thing is done through the vehicle of a story."[27]

(4) The children's story should include fantasy and imagi-

nation.[28] Bruno Bettelheim in Uses of Enchantment credits the

fantasy and imagination (of the fairy tale in particular) with

great importance in the psychological development of the young

child. Ruth Viguers wrote, "Without imagination man cannot

---

[24]Quarterly Review, 1844, p. 4.

[25]Katherine Paterson, "Sounds in the Heart," Hornbook
LVII (December 1981): 781.

[26]Quarterly Review, 1844, p. 7.

[27]Hillaire Belloc, "Children's Books," Living Age 276
(January 18, 1913): 188.

[28]Quarterly Review, 1844, p. 8.

realize full humanity."[29]

(5) Writing for children must be "true to nature."[30] In other words there must be an "inner authenticity."[31] The setting, the characters, the plot--whether a fantasy tale or a factual story--must be realistic. The characters must have a vitality of their own, wrote Miss Annie Moore, so that they can seemingly come to life without the aid of the author's ink.[32] The plot and setting must be real enough to create a concrete world the child can enter. And it must be appealing with "lively incidents" and "dramatic climax"[33] so that the child will want to stay.

In essence, these reviewers are discussing style, theme, plot, and characterization, the major elements in any literary work. In the children's book, the style should not be condescending in nature. The theme may very well be infused with morals, but this should be a natural outgrowth of the story. The style should be imaginative, sketching out scenes, but not coloring in every detail and line. Fantasy, whether it be defined as the imaginative wanderings of the mind or as a specific magical inclusion of a "fairy-tale" element or person, is

---

[29]Doris M. Cole, ed., The Reading of Children: A Symposium (New York: Charles Scribner's Sons, 1932), p. 25.

[30]Quarterly Review, 1844, p. 16.

[31]Elinor Field, ed., Hornbook Reflections: 1949-1966 (Boston: The Horn Book, 1969), p. 70.

[32]Annie E. Moore, "The Reviewing of Children's Books," Bookman 61 (May 1925): 326.

[33]Moore, My Roads to Childhood, p. 26.

an important stylistic inclusion. Also, plot and characters
should be authentic, with the characters coming to life on
their own, and the plot realistic and interesting enough to
draw the child into the story, and to keep him there. It is
these four criteria--plot, style, theme, and characterization--
which will be used in the critical analyses of the five selected late eighteenth century British didactic children's books.

One last point needs to be clarified before the reviewing
commences. Didactic literature, the genre in which these five
books belong, must be defined. Didactic literature is defined
as writing primarily designed to teach moral, ethical or religious issues. Crucial to this definition is also the intention
of the author. Essentially all literary works are created to
communicate an idea, a teaching, an attitude, a fact, an emotion. Only when the author views the function of his writing
as an instructional one, does the book properly qualify as didactic. A result of this pedagogic purpose and inherent in the
definition is that the lessons communicated take precedence
over the book's other artistic qualities.[34] Fabulous Histories, Evenings at Home, The Parent's Assistant, Jemima Placid,
and The Life and Perambulations of a Mouse all were specifically written to teach the child reader proper behaviors, virtues, and deportment.

---

[34]William Thrall and Addison Hubbard, A Handbook to Literature, revised by C. Hugh Holman (New York: Odyssey, 1960),
pp. 144-145.

A Literary Analysis of Fabulous Histories

Dicky, Robin, Pecksy and Flapsy were four nestlings who came into being through the pen of Mrs. Trimmer in 1786. Their purpose in life--to teach the young reader in eighteenth century England the proper treatment and attitudes towards animals. Lest any of the printed word be wasted, Mrs. Trimmer also included in the two hundred pages of Fabulous Histories, lessons on filial obedience, proper manners befitting a guest, accepting one's station in life, the "divine principle of Universal Benevolence" and sibling love. She warned against the dangers of jealousy, gluttony, gossip, keeping bad company, vanities of life, and idle chatter. There is no guile or subtlety in these teachings. Very clearly as the situation arose, the parent birds gave lectures on appropriate attitudes and behaviors. If a situation did not arise, in the tradition of Rousseau, the parent birds would construct one so their offspring would gain an ever wider knowledge of the world around them, and the moral behaviors necessary to live properly within that world.

These lessons were also repeated. As every good teacher knows, and Mrs. Trimmer was a true pedagogue, the lessons need to be presented on the appropriate level and be reviewed in a variety of ways. Since the young child's closest reference point is often the family, the Benson household was quickly introduced. Thus, the various paradigms could be taught by both sets of parents, human and bird. The relationship between the human and feathered families was close, both in outlook of

life and physical proximity. The nest was on the Benson estate, and the young Bensons, Harriet and Frederick, fed the
elder Robins regularly. There is also no doubt that Mr. and
Mrs. Redbreast were as upper middle class in attitude as their
human counterparts.

Other characters also emerged to teach the reader. Mrs.
Trimmer imported the American mocking bird to show the error of
mindless imitation, the magpies to act as a reminder against
idle chatter, the pheasants for vanity, the bees for industry.
The cuckow was given the role as the unwanted and indecorous
foreigner and the poor sparrow was cast as the "wrong sort of
companion." In order that the book not fall entirely in the
realm of the imaginative, humans played an equally important
role in the teachings. To expand the major theme, Mrs. Trimmer
created three families--the Jenkins, the Addises, and the Wilsons.
Oddly reminiscent of Goldilocks' reactions to the beds of the
three bears, the first was too hard in their treatment of animals, the second was too soft, and the third was just right.

Master Jenkins in particular performed atrocities upon the
animal kingdom. He regaled the young Bensons with his horror
stories of pulling wings off of insects, drowning puppies,
throwing cats out of windows, and inciting animals to fight and
mutilate each other. (To give some explanation of how a child
so young could behave so barbarously, Mrs. Trimmer wrote that
Mrs. Jenkins had died when the children were quite young. Thus
Master Jenkins and his sister Lucy never had the opportunity to
receive maternal instruction, so essential to the development

of character.) Through the Bensons' solicitous and constant
admonitions, Miss Lucy saw the errors of her ways and never
again treated animals unjustly. Master Jenkins was past the
point of rehabilitation and "by the time he became a man, had
so hardened his heart, that no kind of distress affected him
. . . consequently, he was despised by all with whom he had any
intercourse." His end came when whipping his steed to go
faster, the horse threw him and Jenkins "was killed on the
spot."

On the other extreme was Mrs. Addis, an individual so en-
raptured with animals that her sensibilities were blinded to
all else. Her own children received no maternal love or physical attention. Her son was sent off to school, her little
daughter kept in rags. The menagerie of cats, dogs, monkeys,
and exotic birds were lavishly fed and doted upon while the
poor were turned away hungry from her door. The scene at the
Addis home was bleak, the stay a lengthy one. Mrs. Benson
noted her daughter's discomfort, so the following discourse was
presented to both Harriet and the young reader as the rationale.

> I know what opinion you have formed of Mrs.
> Addis, and should not have brought you the spec-
> tor of her follies, had I not hoped that an hour
> or two passed in her company would afford you a
> lesson which might be useful to you through life.
> I have before told you that our affections to-
> wards the inferior parts of creation should be
> properly regulated; you have, in your friend Miss
> Jenkins and her brother, seen instances of cru-
> elty to them, which I am sure you will never be
> inclined to imitate; but I was apprehensive you
> might fall into the contrary extreme, which is
> equally blamable. Mrs. Addis, you see, has abso-
> lutely transferred the affection she ought to
> feel for her child, to creatures who would really
> be happier without it.

The third family introduced to the Benson children were
the Wilsons. This hard working farm family not only demonstrated exemplary treatment of pigs, cows, bees, cats, dogs,
donkeys, ducks, chickens, geese, sheep and fish, but also gave
encyclopedic information on the uses of the animals, humane
slaughter, sheep shearing, the care and feeding of domestic
stock, and bee keeping. Through their discussions and behavior,
the rewards of hard work and the Biblical hierarchy of G-d and
his creatures were taught. Mr. Wilson was the epitome of the
virtuous, industrious farmer. Mrs. Wilson was the model of a
good farmer's wife. The children were ideal in manner and
dress. Unfortunately their goodness did not radiate, but came
through like a winter storm.

If this didacticism was all there was to the story, Fabulous Histories would have quickly disappeared in the nineteenth
century. But this was not the case. It was printed up to
1914, if not longer. The fact is, with the exception of the
chapter on the Wilsons, this is a good story to read. Around
the pedantry is a plot well constructed with elements of drama
and suspense. Many of the episodes and incidents are readily
identifiable to the young child. The lessons throughout the
book are given gently. Mrs. Trimmer stresses that if one sees
the errors in his ways and willingly corrects them, everything
will be just fine. This is a far cry from the children's literature of the Puritans that preached damnation as the end result of evil, the reward for good being an early death and
everlasting salvation. Also this book is written well.

Stylistically there are beautiful passages. The story opens as
follows:

> In a hole, which time had made in a wall
> covered with ivy, a pair of REDBREASTS built
> their nest. No place could have been better
> chosen for the purpose; it was sheltered from the
> rain, skreened from the wind, and in an orchard
> belonging to a gentleman who strictly charged his
> domestics, not to destroy the labours of those
> little songsters, who chose his ground as an
> asylum.
> In this happy retreat, which no idle school-
> boy dared to enter, the Hen Redbreast laid four
> eggs, and then took her seat upon them; resolv-
> ing, that nothing should tempt her to leave the
> nest, til she had hatched her infant brood. Her
> tender mate every morning brought her food, be-
> fore he tasted any himself, and then cheered her
> with a song.

This is a very inviting scene. The setting is domestic, one in
which the child reader would feel safe and comfortable. When
the eggs hatched, the mother "with inexpressive tenderness . . .
spread her maternal wings to cover them." In a sense, the
story surrounds the child with maternal love. Mrs. Trimmer
wrote this story originally for her own children. Her devotion
to them as well as to all children was real, and consistently
comes through in the story. The writing waxes poetic at times.
The birds fell "into a gentle slumber, and perfect quietness
reigned . . . ." The mother awoke her young with these words,
"Come my little ones, shake off your drowsiness." And the language is at times imaginative. When Mrs. Wilson opened the
gate to the meadow to let her flock of geese and chickens out,
"the whole party collected, and ran into it like a troop of
schoolboys into their playground."

This book however would yet have failed if its only

redeeming qualities were poetic style and gentle setting. The
child needs suspense and drama in his reading even more than
the adult. Mrs. Trimmer understood this and scattered throughout the story, exciting subplots. In one episode, the parent
birds return to the nest to find their young in a terrible
state of turmoil and fear. The nestlings explained that they
saw a "Monster":

> Suddenly we heard a noise against the wall,
> and presently a great round red face appeared be-
> fore the nest, with a pair of enormous staring
> eyes, a very large beak, and below that a wide
> mouth, with two rows of bones, that looked as if
> they could grind us all to pieces in an instant.
> About the top of his round face, and down the
> sides, hung something black, but not like
> feathers.

The drama is further heightened by the father heroically crying
out, "Never fear!" and flying off to solve the mystery. This
is a delightful piece of writing. It is suspenseful, imaginative, and a fine literary device. The reader is brought into
the tiny bird's nest, and sees his fellow man in a new dimension. Of course in the late eighteenth century, there could
not be an inclusion of a real monster, so Mrs. Trimmer rationally and almost tongue in cheek tells her young reader, "Whilst
these terrible commotions passed in the nest, the monster, who
was no other than honest Joe, the gardener, went to the house
. . . to tell the [Benson] children about the nest."

Mrs. Trimmer recognizes the points of high interest in the
story and often prolongs the suspense by breaking off from the
adventure, switching to another scene. The most exciting part
of Fabulous Histories, from which the author deftly shifts back

and forth, is when the fledglings learn to fly. There is always apprehension in trying the unknown, and leaving the nest literally and figuratively is fraught with conflict. Mrs. Trimmer then adds more to this already dramatic situation. After the young birds safely made the arduous trip from nest to ground, the father commenced his instructions on the art of flying upward for the return flight. Dicky, feeling obstinate and overly confident, refused to listen to his father's advice. Angry with his stubborn behavior, the parents left their wayward youngster to his follies. After many attempts, young Dicky managed to get airborne, but could not find his way back to the nest.

> Sometimes [he] turned to the right, and sometimes to the left; now he advanced forward a little and now, fearing he was wrong, came back again; at length quite spent with fatigue, he fell to the ground and bruised himself a good deal; stunned with the fall, he lay for some minutes without sense or motion but soon revived; and finding himself in this dismal condition, the horrors of his situation filled him with dreadful apprehension.

The elder Robins were good parents and had been watching their son unobserved. Quickly they came to his aid. Since Dicky could no longer fly, a refuge was found for him in the gardener's shed. There he passed his recuperation in relative safety and comfort, with frequent visits from his family. The lesson taught in this adventure is one of filial obedience. If Dicky had not been willful and had listened to the sagacity of his parents' advice, he would never have been lost or injured. This is not what really holds the reader interest. Real worry and concern are generated over the well being of the little bird.   Dicky never fully recovered from his fall.   Although he did eventually fly again, it was not with strength and nimbleness.   The Bensons gave him shelter and food, helping but never caging him.   This permanently cemented the bond between the two families.

The appeal of this book is furthered by Mrs. Trimmer's knowledge of children, their moods and behaviors.   She creates situations which the young reader would easily identify with. In one chapter, the nestlings were fighting about the overcrowding in the nest.   They were pecking each other, kicking, and generally being nasty.   The problem was further compounded when Robin began to order his younger nest mates about, claiming that it was his right as the eldest.   Whether it be in a 1982 Toyota or a 1792 carriage, a small room on a rainy day, or just when everyone is tired, children confined in a small space will fuss with one another.   And how many times are younger siblings reminded that they are not entitled to the rights and privileges of the eldest?   Or what child, after being reprimanded, cannot identify with Dicky's immortal words, "I'll never ever do that again."   Many a mother has heard verbatim these words spoken by their children, and it is highly probable that Mrs. Trimmer heard them from hers.   These words show the author's intuitive understanding of the nature of children: their mercurial temperament, being ever so good one moment, naughty the next, and then, once more, changing back to the angelic.

The book also shares with the child his sense of wonder at

the new and unseen. When the young birds took their first extended flight, they were dazzled by the world around them. "The orchard itself appeared to them a world. For some time each remained silent, gazing around, first at one thing, then at another; at length Flapsy cried out, 'What a charming place the world is.'" This sense of wonder, of seeing the world so freshly, is an integral part of how we define "the essence of childhood."

Mrs. Trimmer also understood the best of the parent-child relationship, its loving and supportive nature. In a lesson on gluttony, Mrs. Benson says to Frederick,

> Do you not recollect one of your acquaintances, who, if an apple-pie, or anything else that he calls nice, is set before him, will eat til he makes himself sick? Frederick looked ashamed, being conscious that he was too much inclined to indulge his love of delicacies. Well, said his mama, I see you understand who I mean, Frederick, so we will say no more on that subject; only when you meet with that little Gentleman, give him my love, and tell him, I beg he will be as moderate as his Redbreasts.

In this little scene we see what Driekers and other modern education psychologists call the "recognition reflex" as well as Thomas Gordon's paradigm of punishing the behavior, but reinforcing the love for the whole child. Here Frederick learned his lesson, but at the same time knew of his mother's love for him.

Also present are real characters. Much of the didactic literature is notorious for its one dimensional characters who exist only to teach the lesson. In Fabulous Histories such characters as Mistress Harriet and the Jenkins children are such examples. Dicky, however, and Frederick in particular, go well beyond this. There is flesh and blood to Frederick, he has a life of his own. As seen in the preceding quotation he has real psychological responses. He is a little boy, who earnestly tries to be good, but is not always successful. He is enthusiastic, impatient, and eager to embrace life's adventures. When he and his sister were first being led to the nest of the robins, his enthusiasm was so great "that he could scarcely be restrained from running all the way." Although he tried to listen dutifully to his mother's advice, he often got sidetracked. Mrs. Trimmer had to admit "I am sorry to say, Frederick was more intent on opening the window, than on imbibing the good instructions that were given to him." Frederick may very well be the first real child found in a book written specifically for the juvenile audience.

Despite the outdated language and the presence of the didactic style, Fabulous Histories is a good book. The story is fast moving (if one skims over the lengthy adult lectures, which perhaps the children did), with suspense and high interest. Appealing details are included in the life of the birds which brings the reader even closer into their feathered world. The Bensons, if not always immensely interesting, are good and loving, offering the child a picture of the best in upper middle class eighteenth century domesticity. The tales of the two families are artfully interwoven. In the hands of a less skilled writer, the story would have been disjointed and cumbersome. But in this book, the reader moves easily from one

setting to the other. He is as comfortable in the Bensons'
drawing room as he is in the nest of the robins. The child
reader is given characters with whom he can identify, as in
Frederick, and ones he can trust, such as Mrs. Benson. Despite
the protest of many modern critics, Fabulous Histories does
indeed fulfill the requirements of children's literature. It
is an enjoyable, well written book, with episodes identifiable
with the child's interests, and aids in his growth as a future
member of society. When one carefully reads this little volume,
it is readily understandable why it had such a long life span.
Fabulous Histories should be considered a milestone in the development of children's literature.

A Literary Analysis of Evenings at Home

Housed in Evenings at Home are imaginative stories, didactic tales, allegories, fables, a fairy tale of sorts, ethno-
graphic studies, poems, plays, farm journals and lessons on
animal behavior, biology, botany, chemistry, philosophy, history, navigation, ship building, economics, geography and geol-
ogy. It is no wonder that these volumes were a mainstay in
nursery libraries in the late eighteenth and nineteenth centuries. They contained a wealth of information and a range of
stories that would appeal to all children, and comprehensively
fulfilled the parent's criteria for suitable, non-frivolous
juvenile literature. This variety in style, theme, and subject
matter was indeed the authors', Dr. Aiken's and Mrs. Barbauld's
purpose in compiling this work. They wanted the children to be

able to pick and choose (to "rummage the budget" as was the expression in the 1700's), depending on mood or inclination, and find reading material for both their amusement and intellectual growth.

It is a book of not only enormous variety, but also of quality. Dr. Aiken was a recognized scholar and presented the most up-to-date scientific facts in his part of the book. Mrs. Barbauld, an already accomplished and well respected poetess and children's writer, lent her talents for the more poetic and imaginative parts. Both authors had considerable experience with children and were respected pedagogues in England at the time. They knew what held children's interest. They were also well versed in the contemporary educational theories. _Evenings at Home_, more directly than the other books selected for this study, reflects the influences of Locke, Edgeworth, and Rousseau. Locke maintained that fables were the proper literary diet to feed children. _Evenings at Home_ very neatly opens with four little fables. Mr. Edgeworth stressed the importance of imaginative play in the development of children. Throughout the book the authors included plays and dialogues to be acted out and imaginative stories to stretch the child's mind.

It is Rousseau's philosophy, however that is most strongly seen. The omnipresent Rousseau tutor is a frequent character in the stories and lessons, following the model established in _Emile_. The tutor should follow his student's lead, wrote Rousseau. So the tutors in _Evenings at Home_ awaited for the student's interest to be demonstrated and awakened. As one tutor exclaimed, "Nothing is so great an encouragement to a tutor as to find his pupils of their own accord seeking after useful information." Although direct teaching (i.e., classroom and textbook learning) was forbidden, it was within the realm of the tutor according to Rousseau to structure situations so that the young protege's attention would be directed to beneficial activities. Thus, in one story a tutor suggests, "Let us sit down awhile on this bench, and look about us. What a pleasant prospect!" The young tutees admire the beauty of the scene but wonder "what a dark, gloomy wood that is at the back of the house." The students picked up on what the mentor wished, the scene was now set for a discourse on the Pine tree and the Fir--the botanical aspects as well as their use and function. Even the most famous of all literary Roussean tutors, Mr. Barlow (created by Rousseau's disciple Thomas Day for Sandford and Merton) enters one dialogue by name to mentor two boys.

Rousseau's concept of the "noble savage" also finds a place in Evenings at Home. In the story of "The Kidnappers," an historical event is related about how the Danes (i.e., civilized man) went into "barbarous" Greenland, taking some of the natives back to Denmark as prisoners. The children in the story questioned if there is a difference between men of culture and those who are considered uncivilized. The mentor replied:

> I know no important difference between ourselves, and these people we are pleased to call savages but in the degree of knowledge and virtue possessed by each. And I believe that many indi-

> viduals among the Greenlanders . . . exceed in
> these respects, many among us. In the present
> case, I am sure the Danish sailors showed them-
> selves the greater savages.

Today, most of the information given so meticulously by
these Rousseau tutors is curiously out of date. The errors are
amusing in their naivete and misconceptions. Yet, despite the
oddity of information given, many of the general explanations
and methods used are clear and appropriate to the cognitive
level of the young child. To describe the difficult principle
of centrifugal force, a tutor explains to a little girl:

> Tutor: You have seen your brother whirl around
>   an ivory ball, tied to the end of a string
>   which he held in his hand . . . .
> Pupil: Yes, and I have done it myself too.
> Tutor: Well then--you felt that the ball was
>   continually pulling, as though it tried
>   to make its escape . . . . Thus you see,
>   there are two powers acting upon the ball
>   at the same time; one to make it fly off,
>   the other to hold it in; and the conse-
>   quence is; that it moves directly accord-
>   ing to neither, but between both; that is
>   round and round.

A science teacher in an elementary school today might give a
very similar explanation. In many respects, Evenings at Home
is like an encyclopedia with its wide range of subjects, but
the entries are more appealing, less formal. As the child
character asks for clarification and expresses his opinions in
the lessons, so the child reader is likewise encouraged to ask
questions about the material. These articles are not just references, they are written in a way to get the child reader actively involved, in the most interesting way possible.

The numerous scientific, historical and philosophical lessons are quite informative and well written, but it is the more

imaginative writings which gave the collection its zest. The
fables in Evenings at Home, although lacking the brilliant imagery and pristine quality of Aesop's, are definitely compa-
rable to Arnold Lobel's collection which won the Caldecott
award in 1980. The didactic tales included are, by their very
nature, heavy in moral overtones, but often the theme goes beyond the rules of eitquette or social attitudes preached in
other eighteenth century children's books. In some of the
stories, the themes could actually be classified as universal,
which is unusual, since much of the didactic literature has
been criticized as being mundane or trivial in theme. In "The
Live Doll," the heroine becomes disenchanted with her doll when
she sees how pale its beauty and function is, compared to many
of the real things in life. Yet, despite looking through
meadow and countryside, she cannot find anything that offers
her steady companionship and love. The story ends when she
"found something which was beautiful as spring flowers, as
gentle and happy as the free bird, as gay as the sportive
lambs, and which better still endowed with a mind and reason
like her own to rejoice in all that is bright, and beautiful,
and good upon earth." It was a baby.

To the modern critic, this may seem soppish, but it is a
real breakthrough in children's literature. The moral of this
didactic piece is dealing with universal themes--the inherent
goodness of man, the beauty of life itself, the kinship that
links the brotherhood of man. This is far superior to lessons
on filial devotion and obedience, and goes beyond the mundane

episodes of children squabbling over a new toy or a window
seat, morals so common in eighteenth century stories for children. Also important to note is the very romantic image of
childhood presented. The baby is shown as good, innocent, and
pure. In Images of Childhood, Peter Coverly suggests that this
romantic ideal, coming from Rousseau, acted as a stimulus for
the brilliance of much of the late Victorian, and post-Victorian
literary masterpieces.

Another example of a moral lesson that goes beyond the didactic is in the dialogue entitled "The Two Robbers." In it, a
Thracian prisoner is brought before Alexander the Great. After
his crimes of murder, plunder and pillage were announced, the
following conversation ensued between the two men:

> Thracian: Have not you, too gone about the
> earth, like an evil genius, blasting
> the fair fruits of peace and indus-
> try;--plundering, ravaging, killing,
> without law, without justice . . . .
>
> Alexander: But, if I have taken like a king, I
> have given like a king. If I have
> subverted empires, I have founded
> greater. I have cherished arts, com-
> merce, and philosophy.
>
> Thracian: I too, have given freely to the
> poor . . . . I have established
> order and discipline . . . and have
> stretched out my protecting arm over
> the oppressed. I know, indeed, lit-
> tle of the philosophy you talk of;
> but I believe neither you nor I shall
> ever repay to the world the mischiefs
> we have done it.
>
> Alexander: Are we, then so much alike? Alexan-
> der, too, a robber? Let me reflect.

This theme--the horrors of war--goes far beyond the usual motives set forth in the didactic mode. Although the child appeal may not have been particularly strong, the fact remains

that an effort was made to bring universal themes to the child reader.

There are two other didactic stories in the collection which are pertinent to the discussion. Although they are far more conventional in theme, the presentation is unusually imaginative. One is "Order and Disorder: A Fairy Tale." One may be reassured that this did not rock the sensibilities of the rational late eighteenth century parent, despite its subtitle. This is a true didactic tale, involving a little girl named Juliet who was very messy and disorderly. She was not making any improvements in her habits, so her mother sent her to an old woman in the village, known to be quite strict. There she was to learn the virtues of an orderly mind and orderly habits.

So far this is the perfect didactic story. There is no characterization, no setting, just a series of episodes exemplifying the virtues of the good trait and the evils of the bad. But in this tale, Mrs. Barbauld managed to slip in two fairy creatures. One was "Disorder," a nasty little thing with messy uncombed hair, torn and rumpled clothes, who set before our heroine tasks that were impossible to complete because of the disarray of equipment and materials. The other sprite was "Order," who "was as upright as an arrow, and not so much as a hair out of place, or the least article of her dress rumpled or discomposed." With a wave of her fairy wand, "Order" was able to organize the task so that Juliet could finish it straightaway. The story is highly imaginative and is structured in a manner very reminiscent of the traditional fairy tale. The child could have in this story the best of both worlds: she could learn the importance of being neat while being transported to the world of make believe.

One of the best remembered stories from the compendium is "The Transmigrations of Indur." Here the theme presented is of benevolence toward animals, a typical one found in much of the contemporary children's literature--but this story is by no means an ordinary one. For one thing, the setting is far removed from the English countryside and middle class parlors. The story takes place in India "at a time when Fairies and Genii possessed the powers which they have now lost." A Brahman by the name of Indur spent his days "exercising his benevolence toward animals in distress." In one of these exercises, he saved a monkey from the clutches of a snake. Indur did not move away quickly enough and received the venomous bite originally intended for the primate. As he lay dying, the monkey turned into a fairy and granted him a last wish in payment for saving her life. He requested that his future lives be spent with his human intellect intact so that he could better appreciate and understand the animals. With the wish granted, Indur went through a succession of lives from a rabbit to an elephant, whenever possible aiding his fellow creatures. He also witnessed the cruelties man imposed on the animal kingdom.

The story is written with a magical quality. The action is fast paced, the drama high as Indur lives through his various existences. The theme is a moral one, the characters flat, yet within this didactic tale, there are no lectures, no contrived episodes. The moral becomes an outgrowth of the story, rather than being superimposed upon it. The imaginative and fairy tale quality of these two stories were exceedingly rare in the eighteenth century. Perhaps Mrs. Barbauld was allowed these flights of fantasy because she was so well respected and because these stories were overshadowed by the other 96 stories in the book.

A far more acceptable and common imaginative outlet in eighteenth century children's literature were the animal stories. Mrs. Trimmer and Miss Kilner were quite successful in this literary mode, and Dr. Aiken followed their lead by writing some delightful sketches of various animals and their responses to man and his world. Not only do the stories allow the child insights into the animal kingdom, but they also show the child different perspectives on life. In one of the fables, a young mouse spies a contraption and cries,

> Mother! the good people of this family have built
> me a house to live in . . . . I am sure it is
> for me, for it is just big enough; the bottom is
> wood, and it is covered all over with wires; and
> I dare say they have made it on purpose to screen
> me from that terrible cat . . . and they have
> been so good as to put in some toasted cheese . . . .

Fortunately for the little mouse, his mother quickly corrected his misconception and explained that this was not a generous gift of lodging but a trap of destruction.

In another story, the reader listens as a mouse tells of his travels around the world. One particularly exciting and harrowing adventure was told as follows:

> I came upon a wide open plain . . . the hard soil
> was every where with huge stones . . . . As I

> was toiling onwards, I heard a rumbling noise be-
> hind me, and with the utmost horror beheld a pro-
> digious rolling mountain approaching me so fast,
> that it was impossible to get out of the way . . . .
> The mountain passed over me and . . . when I re-
> covered . . . to my surprise found myself not in
> the least injured . . . .

This type of writing is not only amusing, but it also ex-
pands the child's mind by asking him to construct a mental picture so that he can learn what, in reality, is the prodigious
mountain or the house with which the mouse was so pleased.

Another example of a story which actively involved the
child and had him draw his own conclusions is in an ethno-
graphic story called "Travellers' Wonders." In this, Captain
Compass describes a culture he has visited, but he does not
mention its name. The captain describes the natives "clad
partly in the skins of beasts made smooth and soft by a particular art, but chiefly in garments made from the outer covering
of a middle sized quadruped, which they are so cruel as to
strip his back while he was still alive." For food, "they were
fond of daubing over [their breads] with a greasy matter that
was the product of a large animal among them . . . . Another
article of food was the curd of milk, pressed into a hard mass
and salted. This had so rank a smell . . . ." Their language
seemed harsh, yet they managed to converse with one another
with ease and fluency. The oddest custom seen by the captain
was the way in which men greeted one another. "Let the weather
be what it will, they will uncover their heads." At this
point, the children in the story as well as the child reader
had guessed the country of these natives.

The lesson allows the child to see his own familiar customs as odd indeed when viewed by a foreigner. It also gives them compassion and understanding for another man's beliefs and habits. Most importantly, it tightly draws the reader into the printed page, keeping him guessing about who these people are, what are these strange foods they eat, the strange clothes they wear. The images presented are riddles, and quite intriguing ones.

Evenings at Home has many of the flaws typically present in late eighteenth century didactic literature. The characterization is almost negligible. Never do we really get to know and understand the motives and personalities of many children and adults who roam through the book. With the exception of "The Transmigrations of Indur," no setting or atmosphere is seen. The major emphasis of the book is one of teaching. Through the didactic tales and the dialogues led by the tutors, the reader could learn about the social mores and attitudes of the day as well as all sorts of scientific and philosophic information. Yet these stories go beyond the norm of the didactic. They draw in the children, actively inviting the readers to think about the stories and themes. And a real fanciful element has crept in, although it is well hidden among the discourses on industry, botany, and history. This gives the book a magical, tantalizing quality. The epilogue contains a poem which hopes that the children will have a better world, one "of light and joy which we, / Alas! in promise only see." Whether the conditions of nineteenth century England were in actuality

better than the preceding one is moot, but unquestionably the
children's literature was lighter and more joyful with imagination given free reign. Evenings at Home holds the promise of
this new style of writing.

A Literary Analysis of The Parent's Assistant

Mr. E. V. Lucas, a literary historian writing at the end
of the last century, called Maria Edgeworth "the first novelist
of the nursery"--a most fitting accolade. Working under the
restraints of both the didactic style and deliberately design-
ing the stories of The Parent's Assistant as a supplement to
the theories in Practical Education, Miss Edgeworth managed to
create a freshness and literary quality never before seen in
books written specifically for children. Even when compared to
the innovativeness of John Newbery's publications, the stories
excel in setting, characterization and complexity of plot. For
the first time, real human characters emerge. So clear are
their motivations and emotions, that even the "bad" characters
solicit sympathy from the reader. The virtuous heroes and
heroines are not merely wished well but actively cheered on by
the reader. In other contemporary eighteenth century didactic
stories, one knows the protagonists will get their just rewards. In Miss Edgeworth's stories, one assumes this will happen, but the reader is not absolutely certain. The predict-
ableness of Fabulous Histories and Jemima Placid is not present
in The Parent's Assistant. The reader has to wait till the
very last pages to find out for certain if virtue will triumph

over evil.

The most consistent attribute in these stories is their complexity of plot. In the stories in Evenings at Home and in the novels of Mrs. Trimmer and the Kilners, the plots are quite simplistic in nature and straightforward. Very easily one episode could be lifted out of the book and stand on its own as a brief moral lesson or fable. This is not the case for the stories in The Parent's Assistant. Each episode is woven from the details and events of preceding ones, leading to further problems or triumphs. The story of "Waste Not, Want Not," although didactic in nature, holds the reader's attention because of just this quality, the intricacy of its story line. The tale opens with Mr. Gresham inviting his two ten-year-old nephews to his home. Hal "passed the first years of his childhood [learning] to waste more of everything than he used." The other nephew, Benjamin, "on the contrary had been taught habits of care and foresight." The scene is clearly set, the reader knows which nephew is the protagonist, which the antagonist, and exactly what the moral of the story will be. What captures the reader's attention are two pieces of string that are mentioned in the beginning of the tale. The boys were given presents. Hal impatiently cuts the string of his package, while Benjamin carefully unknots his, winds it up and puts it away in his pocket. Hal simply cannot understand this demonstration of thrift.

These pieces of string keep reappearing throughout the story. Hal's discarded but not forgotten piece was the cause of his little cousin, Patty, badly spraining her ankle. The string was tangled on a banister. Patty tripped over it, and fell down the stairs. Ben's piece, on the other hand, was used repeatedly in beneficial ways. Its most important function came at the end of the story. Hal and Ben had entered an archery contest. Long hours had been spent in practice, and both boys had grown quite proficient in the sport. The day of the contest finally came, Hal and Ben were the last two archers. Hall went up to the range. He shot his first arrow which landed just a quarter of an inch from the leader's, the proud and wealthy Master Sweepstakes. Upon his second try, his bow string broke and he was disqualified. Up stepped Ben. His first arrow went wild, his second fell next to Ben's. As he placed his third and last arrow in the bow, his string broke also.

> Master Sweepstakes clapped his hands with loud
> exultations . . . [but] our provident hero calmly
> drew from his pocket an excellent piece of string.
> 'The everlasting whip-cord, I declare!' exclaimed
> Hal when he saw it was the very same that had
> tied up the parcel.

With the new string in place, Ben took his last shot and it came closest to the mark, he was the winner.

The author is clearly demonstrating here that one's actions and behaviors do not exist in a vacuum. One event does indeed affect and cause another. Repeatedly in the stories, acts of kindness and honesty set into motion a chain of events which led to rewards, while the acts of dishonor, carelessness and vanity reap their own misfortunes. Miss Edgeworth developed the didactic tale into an effective and forceful teaching instrument. Through the characters and plot, the child reader learned about the ramifications of one's actions. He not only was taught the expected mores and behaviors of his society, but the reason why it was so important to adhere and conform to these rules. These lessons were taught very directly; not through the homilies of the adults, but through the child characters' own words and deeds.

Maria Edgeworth knew that for the morals of her stories to have the most impact, she would have to get the child reader actively involved in the story. She did this by generating considerable suspense in many of the tales. Adventure piles on adventure. The story of "The Little Merchants" is an example of this. Here the reader is introduced to two boys. Francesco, an honest, hardworking lad, and Pietro, a lazy boy who expects the rewards of life to be reaped upon him with little effort on his part. While Francesco earns his living through honesty, Pietro does so by fraud and deception. Francesco, of course, is rewarded for his labors. He is well respected, his fruit business prospers. Pietro is discovered for the rogue that he is. He is banned from the market and even his father, a malcontent and ne'er-do-well, throws him out of the house in disgust.

The story could have easily ended here. There are interesting characters, various and exciting episodes. But the story goes on with vigor. Here, Miss Edgeworth's talents push the story beyond the didactic into a high action tale. Because of his honesty, industry and good nature, Francesco comes to the notice of an Englishman of wealth and position, vacationing in Italy. He apprentices Francesco to a drawing master. The boy studies and draws ancient ruins, demonstrating considerable talent. While working at the ancient site, he noticed that one of the nearby wells is drying up. Knowing that this is a sign of an impending volcanic eruption, he warned the Englishman, his hosts the Count and Contessa and the village. They all escaped with little time to spare, for within a few days Vesuvius erupted. Returning later to the smoldering, ash covered town, Francesco learns that a stash of gunpowder and fireworks was in the Count's villa. If not drenched in water, it would explode causing even greater destruction. Taking his life in his hands, he brings water up to the villa, and the town is saved.

If all this adventure was not enough, one final subplot emerges. Unfortunately then, as today, looting was rampant in the aftermath of a disaster. Francesco was commissioned to stand guard at the villa. Who now comes upon the scene but Pietro with a band of robbers. Armed with pistols, they plan to steal the wealth hidden below the volcanic debris. As Francesco stands guard unaware, the robbers stealthily approach the villa. Pietro at this point is impatiently awaiting the return of his comrades at the home of the "fence" (for want of a better name). He knows that it is Francesco at the villa. Guilt plagues him, for Francesco has been a good friend. But Pietro is not moved to action; his character is too weak, his fear of the band's revenge too strong. Finally, a series of events forces Pietro to tell the authorities about the impending

robbery. The police rush to the scene of the crime. Francesco
has been wounded, but not seriously. The riches of the villa
were saved, the bandits sent to prison.

Miss Edgeworth developed suspense and dramatic action in
her stories that had not ever been seen in literature specifically for children. This is similar to the drama found in
Robin Hood, stories of the Knights of the Round Table and Robinson Crusoe. The author is bridging the gap between children's and adult's literature. She is taking the best qualities seen in adult fiction, and giving it to the younger reader
in his own special book. She simplified the style and vocabulary, included socializing lessons, created characters and episodes with which the child could identify, accomplishing all
this without sacrificing any of the drama and tour de force so
important in fine writing.

Maria Edgeworth's literary characters are also highly
unique. With rare exception, the characters in eighteenth century didactic children's stories are flat, and created only to
exemplify the evils or virtues preached within the tale. Motivation for behaviors is omitted, the inner workings of the mind
not shown. The characters in The Parent's Assistant break from
this restrictive mold. The reader is shown the thoughts and
feelings of the characters. The result is a greater compassion
and understanding of both the protagonists and antagonists.

An exemplary characterization is seen in the story entitled "Lazy Lawrence." The hero of this tale is Jem, an industrious lad who is earning money to help his bedridden mother

pay the rent. Through hard work, honesty, and ingenuity, he

collects quite a tidy sum. He innocently and with much pride

shows his wealth to Lawrence, who although not a bad boy, was

very lazy, and whose sloth eventually got him involved with a

bad group of boys. Lawrence tells the leader of this band

about Jem's money. The leader slyly suggests that they borrow

a bit of it, and repay the money when they win it back at gam-

bling. The story proceeds as follows:

> In the dead of night Lawrence heard someone tap
> at the window. He knew well who it was, for this
> was the signal agreed upon between him and his
> wicked companion. He trembled at the thoughts of
> what he was about to do . . . .

Upon arriving at the barn which was Jem's hiding place, Law-

rence cried out:

> 'Let us go back, it is time yet'--'It is no time
> to go back,' replied the other, opening the door.
> 'You've gone too far now to go back,' and he
> pushed Lawrence into the stable.

When the cache was found, Lawrence's companion took it all.

> Lawrence cried, 'you said, you'd only take half a
> crown, and pay it back on Monday--You said you'd
> only take half a crown!' 'Hold your tongue,' re-
> plied the other, walking on deaf to all remon-
> strances--'if I am to be hanged, it sha'n't be
> for half a crown.' Lawrence's blood ran cold in
> his veins, and he felt as if all hair stood on
> end.

Once back home,

> Lawrence crept, with all the horrors of guilt
> upon him, to his restless bed. All night he was
> starting from frightful dreams; or else, broad
> awake, he lay listening to every small noise, un-
> able to stir, and scarcely daring to breathe--
> tormented by that most dreadful of all kinds of
> fear, that fear which is the constant companion
> of an evil conscience. He thought the morning
> would never come.

The next day, Jem met Lawrence on the road:

> Jem looked at him and said, 'You look white . . .
> for you've turned as pale as death'--'Pale!', re-
> plied Lawrence, not knowing what he said; and
> turned abruptly away, for he dared not stand
> another look at Jem; conscious that guilt was
> written in his face, he shunned every eye.

This is a compelling piece of writing. The reader is drawn into the story, becoming deeply involved with Lawrence's actions and thoughts. Ever so succinctly and compassionately, Miss Edgeworth describes the awesome fears and confusions of the wrongdoer. Never before in children's literature had such depth of characterization been seen. Never before had the child been allowed so deep and intense an involvement with the "bad" character. Miss Edgeworth has allowed the child to see the hero in action, the bad one--guilt ridden and distraught.

She also created for the first time a child character who consistently and realistically was indeed a child in thought and action. Her name was Rosamond. Introduced in "Rosamond and the Purple Jar" she was so popular that later, a whole series of stories were created about her. Rosamond was chatty, loving, ever so earnest to be good, sometimes naughty, silly, stubborn, and outspoken. It is no wonder that the late eight-eenth and early nineteenth century child adored her so. If she was not the mirror image of themselves, then of someone they knew intimately.

The Edgeworth characters were also unique for besides be-ing industrious, honest and goodnatured, the heroes and hero-ines were also independent, resourceful and creative. The little boy in "The Basket Woman" invented a "scotcher" as he

called it, which was a wedge that prevented carriages from
rolling backwards on an incline. From this venture, the boy
made a fair amount of money. Jem, in "Lazy Lawrence," became
quite adept at making straw mats. Mary, in "The Orphans," designed a bedroom slipper that became quite popular. Soon the
trade became so brisk, she had to hire the village children to
keep up with the demand.

Not only do the child characters in The Parent's Assistant
differ from those in other didactic tales, but the adults in
these stories take on a new role. Usually the parent and adult
in typical eighteenth century children's stories act as the
tutor, training the children, providing examples. In many of
Miss Edgeworth's stories, the parents take a much more subtle
position. They do not lecture, they do not teach. Sometimes
they act as the impetus for development of the child's own talents. If a parent is too ill or some tragedy befalls him and
he can not pay the bills, the job is left to the child's own
inventions. Other times they act as benefactors, reminiscent
of the fairy godmothers in the folk tales. When times become
so bleak that the child hero/heroine cannot possibly overcome
the difficulties, no matter how honest and industrious he may
be, a man or woman of distinction magically comes forward to
help out. Like their fairy godmother prototypes, these benefactors only appear after the child has proven himself honest,
good natured and virtuous. Also, following the tradition established by the fairy godmother, these benefactors provided
aid and support but they never totally solved the child's

problem. The child at the end had to once again demonstrate integrity, strength of character, and overcome the difficulties himself.

Another innovative part of these stories are their settings. The child reader is frequently taken from his middle class parlor to rustic villages and foreign countries. "The Orphans" took place "near the ruins of the castle of Russmore in Ireland." Pietro and Francesco lived in the south of Italy. Simple Susan resided "in a retired hamlet on the border of Wales." These settings are also given in depth. "The Basket Woman" begins:

> At the foot of a steep, slippery, white hill, near Dunstable in Bedfordshire, called Chalk Hill, there is a hut, or rather a hovel, which travelers could scarcely suppose could be inhabited, if they did not see the smoke rising from its peaked roof. An old woman lives in this hovel, and with her a little boy and girl . . . .

This description is so clear in its detail that one could assume that it could be easily located. One wonders if some young child did not urge his parents to search out this humble abode and offer personal assistance.

The rudiments of literary devices to produce atmosphere is also seen in these stories. The night when Lawrence stole Jem's money, "a black cloud was just passing over the moon." The serenity of the English countryside was depicted in "Simple Susan"--"all was silent; the grey light of the morning was now spreading over every object, the sun rose slowly, and Susan stood at the lattice window, looking through the small leaded cross-barred panes at the splendid spectacle." Beautiful

poetic images were written by Mrs. Trimmer and Mrs. Barbauld,
and indeed these added to the quality of their books, but once
again, Maria Edgeworth went further than her predecessors. She
was not just writing poetic metaphors, she created with her
words a three dimensional background into which the child could
enter.

At her best, Maria Edgeworth created stories for The Parent's Assistant that were dramatic and intricate. Suspense and
adventure builds, as the reader turns the pages to see if good
will in truth win over evil. A myriad of characters are developed for the child to identify with, admire, sympathize with,
pity, and at times abhor. At her worst, Miss Edgeworth is didactic, her themes petty. She does not have the confidence in
her writing to let it speak for itself. She intrudes upon her
stories to make editorial comments about the behavior of the
characters, or to discuss an educational theory. A few times,
after describing delightful little incidents she footnoted
them, reassuring the reader that this was a real, true event.
When her stories revolve around competitions in the English
boarding school, the plots weaken. Stories such as "The Bracelots," and "The Barring out" deal with power plays, and mean,
petty behaviors. In real life, such situations are terrible to
be involved with and extremely unpleasant to witness as a by-
stander. To be deliberately brought into such a setting is un-
comfortable. These stories also do not do what good literature
should do--transport the child reader to another place. These
boarding school stories are so realistic, so true to life, the

child is left in one of the nastier places of childhood--on the playing fields watching his peers be vain and cruel.

Despite these weaknesses, The Parent's Assistant is undoubtedly the best of the five selected books. Miss Edgeworth is a master storyteller, her plots dramatic, suspenseful, unpredictable. The characters and settings are three dimensional, inviting the child to step in closer and study the scenes and action. The writing is innovative. The characterization is clear and varied, bringing the child in contact with a whole range of human emotions and conditions. The child not only interacts with the well-to-do, but also meets with persons of more humble circumstances. These people of the lower classes are not included to teach lessons about charity, but to show the middle class child that rich and poor share the same feelings.

Perhaps most importantly, these stories exude a positiveness. The child characters in these stories are not mere passive receivers of parental/tutor lectures, nor are they confined to small petty behaviors. The children in The Parent's Assistant are true heroes and heroines. They comfort their sick parents, they pay the rent, they help out siblings and save their pets from slaughter or sale. They show courage, ingenuity, strength of character and determination. These stories offer the child of the late eighteenth century far more than rules for etiquette and moral behavior. They give him a sense of confidence in himself and his abilities. It is this heroic quality, depicted with such drama and realism, that very

well may have been responsible for making these stories popular
for one hundred and fifty years.

A Literary Analysis of The Life and Perambulations of a Mouse

Animals have always been present in literature that children have loved. In myths and legends, in the fairy and folk
tales, talking creatures abound. But in the eighteenth century,
this fantasy world was banished from the nursery shelves. The
three Billy Goats Gruff, Puss in Boots, and Beauty's Beast
were locked away in storage closets and cellars. Newbery and
others tried to bring animals back into children's stories.
They knew how animals could easily capture the child's attention, and that they had the potential of being effective teaching devices. "Histories" of quadrupeds and birds were quite
popular, and the ABC books were often decorated with animal
illustrations. In the emerging juvenile fiction, animals became trusted companions in story-books. One lap-dog by the
name of Pompey had the distinction of being the major character
of a tale. Generally, however, these eighteenth century fictional animals were related to neither the fairy world nor the
naturalistic one. Their purpose was to teach morals and proper
behavior. These characters were not animals dressed in man's
clothes, but rather humans in animal skins. They were devoid
of charm and animal characteristics.

In 1783(?), the Marshall publishing house put The Life and
Perambulations of a Mouse by Dorothy Kilner on the market.
Both the author and her publisher wished to give an appealing

animal story to the child, but one without that "useless trumpery" found in the fairy tale. So, most carefully and distinctly, Miss Kilner told her reading public in the Preface that the primary goal in the book was instructional:

> Before you begin the following history, which is made believe to be related by a MOUSE, I must beg you will be careful to remember, that the author's design in writing it, was no less to instruct and improve, than it was to amuse you. It is, therefore, earnestly hoped, as you read it, you will observe all the good advice there is delivered, and endeavor to profit from it.

This statement seems quite clear, but obviously the author was not totally satisfied that she had stressed the seriousness of the underlying themes. Thus, she reiterated a few pages later:

> But, before I proceed to relate the new companion's history [i.e., the little mouse] I must beg leave to reassure my readers that, in earnest, I never heard a mouse speak in all my life . . . and only wrote the following narrative as being far more entertaining, and not less instructive, than my own [history] would have been.

Miss Kilner seems to be protesting a bit too much. One might assume that the author was very much aware of her story's imaginative and appealing qualities, and was fearful that the educational value would be lost. In truth, Miss Kilner created a highly innovative, charming story. She gave to young readers an animal character which was true to the natural temperament and habits of the animal. Miss Kilner also created a bond between the animal and the reader through shared emotions and adventures. Nimble, Brighteyes, Softdown, and Longtail, the four mice brothers in this story are the prototypes for the wonderful animal characters that were to emerge in Sewell's, Beatrix Potter's, Robert Lawson's, and E. B. White's writings.

The child is immediately drawn into the story through its
innovative introduction. The author began: "During a remark-
ably severe winter, when a prodigious fall of snow confined
everyone to their habitations," a large party of young people
(of which the author was a member) gathered for a visit at
Meadow Hall. One "sprightly girl" suggested that each of the
group should "draw up some kind of history" to amuse the rest.
Alone in her room, the author was at loose ends trying to create a "diverting" story. She was hesitant to write her own
life story, "though deeply interesting to myself, [it] will be
insipid and unentertaining to others." While pondering the
situation, she heard a squeaking little voice say, "Then write
mine, which may be more diverting." Looking about, the author
found a mouse by its hole who again requested, "Will you write
my history?" Quite surprised by this request, the author soon
regained her composure and said, "Come, therefore, and sit upon
my table, that I may hear more distinctly what you have to re-
late." The mouse instantly accepted the invitation "and with
all nimbleness of its specie, ran up the side of my chair, and
jumped upon the table; when getting into a box of wafers, it
began" its tale.

This introduction is exceedingly good. The tone is intimate and confiding. The child reader meets the author of the
story who has a problem--how can she best entertain her
friends? To a child, this is a problem completely understandable, quite complex in nature, and of high priority. Now, who
should come to the author's aid, but a mouse. This is

obviously quite an ordinary one (for if he was magical, he would have shrunk the author down to his size or some such stuff), similar to the creatures the child accidentally came across in pantry and closet. The child now had the opportunity to become personally acquainted with one--which is an interesting prospect.

Miss Kilner then develops an emotional bond between the reader and the mouse. Nimble, the name of the mouse-hero, commences his story with his earliest recollection, the day his mother left him and his three brothers, since they had grown big enough to care for themselves. She gives her young final instructions and advice, then "she stroked us all with her fore paw, as a token of her affection, and hurried away, to conceal from us the emotions of her sorrow, at thus sending us into the wide world." The little mice were saddened by the "parting from our kind parent," but "the thought of being our own directors so claimed our little hearts, that we presently forgot our grief." Here important and recognizable emotions are presented, readily identified with: one of maternal love, one of the anguish of separation, and thirdly the excitement of becoming grown up and going off on your own.

But this is the late eighteenth century, where imagination and interest are not allowed to be the sole components in a children's story. Morals and teaching messages also had to be presented, and Miss Kilner took her role as a transmitter of cultural values most seriously. After this imaginative and novel introduction, the author quickly interjected her first lesson. When the four mice were wandering through the parlor of a well-to-do family, the little girl of the house saw the creatures. She became hysterical, shrieking and squealing. Her mother scolded her for such foolish behavior, and then gave her an extended (six page!) lecture on the inanities of displaying fear of animals. Unfortunately the mother's lecture was as silly as her daughter's behavior. The mother spoke of a young woman who was severely burned, stricken with pneumonia, and nearly drowned--all caused by overwrought, irrational responses to animals. The last episode recounted was when the girl, frightened by a wasp, jerked her head backwards and went through a glass window. Large pieces of glass became stuck in her neck, causing much pain and a severe loss of blood.

Fortunately for the reader most of the lessons are taught by Nimble, who is far more sensible and rational than the aforementioned mother. He is also more concise and succinct. He teaches the child reader about the importance of filial devotion, being content with one's station in life, the joys of a happy heart versus material riches, civility in manners, and proper treatment of animals. Many of the episodes in which these lessons are taught are interesting, with adventure and suspense. In one vignette, Miss Kilner develops atmosphere, which is quite rare in late eighteenth century writing. In this scene, Nimble and his brother are searching for a new home.

> The night was very dark and tempestuous: the
> rain poured down in torrents; and the wind blew
> so exceeding high . . . it was with difficulty we
> could keep our legs . . . . The spattering of

> the rain, the howling of the wind, together with
> the rattling and shaking of the trees, all con-
> tributed to make such a noise as rendered it im-
> possible for us to hear whether any danger was
> approaching or not.

This is fine imaginative writing which builds up the suspense
of the scene. The reader is drawn into the story and becomes
actively concerned with the welfare of the two mice.

The mice brothers find themselves in various predicaments,
often where life and limb are threatened. The author builds up
drama, and even a bit of humor is seen at times. One example
is when the mice are surprised by the owners of the home. Not
knowing where to hide, Nimble relates:

> We ran up the back of the lady's gown, by which
> means she lost sight of us, and gave us an oppor-
> tunity to make our escape, as she opened the door
> to order the cat to be brought in. We seized the
> lucky moment, and dropping from the gown, fled
> with utmost haste . . . .

Not only is there a bit of slapstick here, but it is also an
exciting escape.

The author, however, was at her best when she described
the love and comradeship between the brother mice. When
Softdown was caught in a trap, Nimble said:

> It is impossible to describe our consternation
> and surprise upon this occasion, which was
> greatly increased when we advanced near the
> place, at seeing him (through some little wire
> bars) confined in a small box, without any vis-
> ible way for him to get out, and hearing him in
> the most moving accepts beg us to assist him in
> procuring his liberty.

The three mice tried to gnaw through the wood and liberate
their brother, but were chased away from their endeavors by a
human. Although they deeply grieved for their brother, they

had to flee for their own safety. The reader feels sympathy
not only for the caged mouse but also for his brothers who
despite their efforts could not save him.

Another example of fraternal devotion and affection was
shown when Nimble was comforted by his brother. Nimble had
barely escaped the tortures of two boys, and had witnessed the
death of his brother, Brighteyes. He was grief stricken and
exhausted. Longtail begged his brother to calm himself and
rest.

> So, my dear Nimble, endeavor to compose yourself,
> and take a little rest after the pain and fatigue
> which you have gone through, otherwise you may be
> sick; and what will become of me, if any mischief
> should befall you? I shall then have no brother
> to converse with; no friend to advise me what to
> do! Here he stopped, overpowered with grief for
> the loss of our two murdered brothers, and with
> his tender solicitudes for my welfare.

The caring, the respect, the sorrow is poignant and handled
with sensitivity. (The language may seem pedantic and stiff to
us, but these were the speech patterns of the eighteenth century, a time period known for its extended and sentimental
expressions.)

Through Miss Kilner's descriptions and dialogues, a real
caring and concern is generated for the mice, and in particular, Nimble. The reader is made aware of his attachment for
the mouse, when three-quarters of the way through the book,
Nimble is frightened away when a maid enters the room. This is
an unexpected turn of events. The reader anxiously awaits the
return of Nimble, but he does not show up despite the female
character laying tasty morsels in front of his hole. Not only

is the reader concerned for the mouse's safety, but one is
wrapped up enough in the story to want to hear the conclusion
of Nimble's tale. The mouse is eventually found--but in a half
dead condition. He had fallen into a large ceramic jar of
"Turkey figs" and was unable to get out. The young lady nursed
him back to health, and then, to everyone's relief, Nimble finished the telling of his "history."

The Life and Perambulations of a Mouse does not have the
intricacy of plot or the three dimensional characters found in
Miss Edgeworth's stories. It does not have the gentleness of
mood or imagination found in Fabulous Histories. Neither does
it have the artful merging of the didactic elements with the
story line as seen in some of the tales in Evenings at Home.
But this is an important book in the development of children's
literature. Its importance lies in its novelty of form. This
most probably is one of the first stories written specifically
for children where a wild animal (rather than a domestic one)
becomes the main character, telling its story in first person.
There is also a uniqueness to the intimate relationship between
the young lady character and Nimble, the teller of the tale.
The female character and mouse are presented almost as equals;
a real respect for the animal is shown. In most late eighteenth century and early nineteenth century stories, humans were
the protectors and benefactors of animals. The creatures were
usually kept in a subservient position.

Also Nimble was characterized not as a child or man in
animal skins. He always remained a mouse, with all of the

mouse's innate characteristics--nimbleness, constant activity, timidness, shyness, a voracious appetite. The fact that he can talk does not at all take away from his animal nature. Nimble's speech is so natural and unassuming, his stories so realistic, that the reader is delighted to become more intimately acquainted with this denizen of the pantry. Nimble is the true ancestor of Peter Rabbit, Benjamin Bunny, Mrs. Tiggy-Winkle, and the other Potter creations. Miss Potter's characters, although extremely verbal and quite stylishly dressed, never stray from their true animal nature or habitat. These, of course, became the prototypes for so many of the later twentieth century animal stories. One wonders if The Life and Perambulations of a Mouse sat upon Miss Potter's nursery bookshelf--this is within the realm of possibility.

A Literary Analysis of Jemima Placid

In the preface of Jemima Placid, the author Mary Jane Kilner wrote that children's lives are not as happy and carefree as we adults suppose. Although we may view their hardships as trifling, the children feel their disappointments as deeply as we adults lament our own misfortunes. To diminish the pain of disappointment, Mrs. Kilner composed this story of a little girl named Jemima Placid who was to show children how their lives could be made more comfortable, if they did not dwell on life's misfortunes. Maintain a happy disposition throughout one's travails and keep things in perspective, the author suggests, and then not only will disappointments fade that much more quickly, but the reader will be admired for a positive outlook on life. The pages in this little volume were written with much earnestness, and with the child's welfare as the major concern.

Despite all of its sincerity, <u>Jemima Placid</u> is not particularly good literature. The story is just what the subtitle suggests: "The Advantage of Good Nature, Exemplified in a Variety of Familiar Incidents." Jemima is confronted with assorted situations in a variety of settings, all established to best demonstrate her sweet nature. The book contains no real drama or suspense. The incidents are rather mundane, the behaviors and outcomes, predictable. The settings are almost nonexistent, with neither descriptive passages, nor atmosphere. The characters are flat, there are no insights into why they behave in the way they do. There are no major character reformations either. The bad children remain naughty, not making any dramatic changes in attitude or behavior. They are not affected by the admonitions from the adults or the perfect example set by Mistress Placid. The theme is not heroic; it is, rather, the simple message that good nature will help overcome the hardships of life. With the exception of one poem, there are no streaks of brilliance in the writing, no imaginative metaphors, no poetic leanings in style.

Yet this book was enjoyed by children. The copy used by this researcher, a third edition published in 1785?, is very worn, obviously having gone through many readings and much handling. The spine is gone. Some past owner carefully

retaped it, and with a childish hand retitled it so that it
could be found more easily on the nursery bookshelf. Despite
the literary failings, this book is not tiresome reading.
There is an intrinsic appeal within its pages. Since the stan-
dard criteria of plot, theme, style, and characterization do
not explain the interest of the book, one must look into the
emotional components which create its reading pleasure.

The key to the book's appeal lies in the fairy tale quality of the book. By fairy tale, it is not meant that there was
an inclusion of a magical tool or fairy tale creature, for that
would never have been acceptable in late eighteenth century
England. Rather, Jemima Placid, herself, seems to be the per-
sonification of Sleeping Beauty, Snow White, Cinderella and the
other heroines which roam the fairy books. All of these characters demonstrate the same basic personality traits of sweetness and patience. It is these traits that result in their
being rewarded in the end. If Cinderella had not gone through
the hardships imposed by her stepmother with an even and loving
temperament, surely, the fairy godmother would not have wrought
her magic and sent her to the ball. The fairy tale heroines
are rewarded not for their external beauty but for their beautiful hearts. For this they are given a prince of a man to
marry, the admiration of all, and a life that promises to continue happily ever after.

Jemima has all of the same personality traits as her fairy
tale predecessors. The reader senses this. Although the book
ends with Jemima being only sixteen, it is known that she will

live happily ever after. She will marry a kind and genteel man, live in comfrotable surroundings, be blessed with happy, healthy children, and be loved by all who know her. This is a certainty, for it is Jemima's just reward. Her "sweetness of manners" and "the even and unruffled serenity of her temper" deserve no less. (Although fairies were officially banned from the late eighteenth century, one should not suppose that children had lost their familiarity with them. The medieval fairy tale was still flourishing in the chapbooks and broadsides, easily purchased from a traveling peddler. Perrault's Tales of Mother Goose was published at the end of the 1600's and was soon after translated into English. Further, it is hard to believe that the nurses and governesses never lapsed into telling a fairy tale at their charge's bedtime.)

Although some modern critics find such heroines soppish, many little girls (and it was for the feminine gender that Jemima Placid was written) love these characters. They model them in their play and use the structure of the fairy tale in their own creative writings. Despite the concerns of liberated men and women, the goals of the fairy tale are not at all superficial--they are instead quite satisfying. Is it so wrong to wish to be respected by others, and live happily ever after? (As far as marrying a prince; it may not be a proper goal for a modern woman, but it does make life easier!) This basic appeal does not stop when adulthood is reached. The modern romances, so popular today, are in reality spiced up fairy tales. The heroines, placed in different time periods and dressed in

different costumes are often sweet, innocent, patient, gentle
and loving. Their personalities as well as their rewards are
reminiscent of fairy tale princesses and youngest daughters.
Jemima Placid, given a more romantic name, could as easily fit
into a Barbara Courtland novel as she could into a medieval
fairy tale.

True fairy tales are stories of high drama. They do not
include day-to-day trivialities. Jemima Placid fills in the
missing gaps. Through Jemima the reader gets a peek at the way
Snow White or Rose Red handled daily life. It is human nature
to want a more intimate knowledge of the rich and famous. Many
a livelihood is made from the writing of gossip columns, inter-
views of current day idols and biographies. These share with
the reader, incidents in the lives of well known personalities,
to which they would never ordinarily be privy. Jemima Placid
is a biography of the early life of a fairy tale heroine.

These fairy tale qualities of the book are very important.
If these, however, were the only positive elements in the
story, the book might not have been as successful as it was.
There are three other components within the story, which keep
alive interest and appeal. One is that the book is short, just
91 pages. It can easily be read in one sitting by a good
reader. The book would have become boring if extended much
more. There is not enough drama that would allow a child to
repeatedly put it down, then resume reading at later times.
Credit should be given to the author for knowing how much the
reader would tolerate and enjoy. Mrs. Kilner could have easily

included additional episodes to demonstrate Mistress Placid's temperament. Also she could have increased the length and frequency of the adults' homilies. But she did not. She knew when to end the book.

Another important aspect of the book is that the incidents and episodes described were indeed "familiar" to the child reader. When Jemima was sent off to London, the parting was a sorrowful one. Yet amidst the tears and the grief, Jemima's little brothers made up a list of things they wished their sister to purchase. Properly, this list in the best of the didactic tradition should have included sensible and instructional items. Instead, Mrs. Kilner included childhood treasures--some Indian glue, skates, a carriage whip. When Jemima most prudently suggested the purchase of a new pencil which was sorely needed, Little Charles responded "no, father would supply that want," and quickly substituted in its place "a gun with a touch-hole."

And then there was the incident of Jemima's cousin who had received a new cap for the upcoming ball. She "went a dozen times in the day to look at [it], wishing it was time to put it on." How many times, in the early stages of ownership, do we peek at a new purchase. Mrs. Kilner's purpose for including this was to show the silliness of vanity. In truth it is a vain behavior, but it is also so very natural. In another scene, Jemima's cousins ended up in a fight over a seat. The younger cousin began most amicably requesting that her sister move over so they could both share the window seat. The elder "very crossly refused" and responded "get another seat for yourself, for you cannot sit here." Anyone accompanying a group of children on a trip has witnessed such a conversation on more than one occasion. Mrs. Kilner knew children--their behaviors, their pleasures, what made them cross, what made them tired. A letter written to Jemima by young Charles ended, "I do not think I have much more to say, for writing is such tedious work that I am quite tired." Recent research in the field of early writing hypothesizes that there are at least ten mental operations utilized by the young child in the early stages of printing and composing. This involves enormous con- centration on the part of the child. Mrs. Kilner understood the implications and conclusions some two hundred years before such research was published. What made her so successful as a children's writer was this insightful understanding of the child.

Although the writing style is not outstanding, the author knew the importance of a good beginning and ending, and had the talent to carry this through. This is the third important com- ponent which makes the book so readable. The story opens, "As I had nothing particular to do, I took a walk one morning as far as Saint James Park, where meeting with a lady of my ac- quaintance, she invited me to go home with her to breakfast." When the two ladies reached their destination, a young daughter asked the author for the particulars of Miss Jemima Placid, since her mama had often alluded to her as a model of perfect behavior. The story that ensued was a direct result of this request. The honesty and naturalness of this opening scene is appealing and invites one to read on. The story basically ends with a delightful poem which sums up the theme of the book with a twinkle in the eye and a bemused grin.

> Nay, Nelly dear! now do not cry,
> And wet that pretty sparkling eye;
> What tho' by chance I tore your lace,
> Don't make that terrible grimace!
> Do put that ugly frown away,
> And join again in social play!
> For, after all, what can you do?
> Will pouting thus the rent renew?
> But Nell, why what a brawl you keep,
> I vow the chickens cannot sleep; . . .
> The horses that were grazing there,
> Have left their food at you to stare.
> Your noise disturbs all nature's peace, . . .
> A needle, with assiduous care,
> May the torn frock again repair;
> But petulance, and passion's strife,
> Will rend the future bliss of life . . . .

Although Jemima Placid has long been discarded from juvenile libraries, it is to be hoped that the author's desire for children's lives to be filled with happiness and contentment will never be forgotten.

CHAPTER V

SUMMARY AND CONCLUSIONS

The Parent's Assistant by Maria Edgeworth, Fabulous Histories by Mrs. Trimmer, Evenings at Home by Mrs. Barbauld and
Dr. Aiken, Jemima Placid by Mary Jane Kilner and The Life and
Perambulations of a Mouse by Dorothy Kilner have been generally
disregarded and/or discredited by modern literary historians.
Their main problem according to the majority of critics, is the
didactic style. Didacticism is viewed as stifling the child's
imagination,[1] and denying the spontaneous nature of childhood.[2]
The insistence upon moral digressions destroys the style and
the plot.[3] The characters in such stories become flat, mere
pawns in the lessons of right versus wrong. The adult-child
narratives are artificial and stiff.[4] As one commentator concluded, didacticism "is contrary to our view of the happy,

---

[1]Roger Lancelyn Green, Tellers of Tales (New York: Franklin Watts, 1965), p. 12.

[2]Paul Hazard, Books, Children and Men (Boston: The Horn
Book, 1947), p. 14.

[3]F. J. Harvey Darton, Children's Books in England: Five
Centuries of Social Life (Cambridge: Cambridge University,
1958), p. 158.

[4]Isabelle Jan, On Children's Literature (London: Bayles
and Son, 1973), p. 23.

relaxed, and more or less equal relationship between the generations which we now regard as ideal."[5] To these modern critics, the inclusion of didacticism in children's literature is wrong. By its very nature, it suppresses the literary merits of the story, destroys any child appeal the book may have, and implies a tense authoritarian parent-child relationship.

Yet, upon careful examination, these five selected books appear not to demonstrate the aforementioned negative qualities supposedly inherent in didactic literature. Sections of the books are beautifully written, with poetic imagery and sensitivity. The plots are suspenseful with dramatic action. Real character development is beginning to emerge. The spontaneity of the child characters is not always drowned in the strictures of the moral overtones. At times, the characters are quite lively and portray real child-like behaviors and motivations. Loving and supportive parent-child relationships are clearly and consistently presented. And imagination has not been banished, for if it was, how could a mouse tell his life story so poignantly, or a family of robins be written about with such charm and appeal.

It is quite obvious that the literary analyses just presented run counter to much of what has been written in the modern histories of children's literature. The differences in the evaluations may be caused by a number of factors. The most

---

[5]John Rowe Townsend, Written for Children: An Outline of English Children's Literature (Philadelphia: Lippincott, 1974), p. 39.

important seems to be that some modern critics tend to pull the
books out of their historical time frame. They have forgotten
that these books, because they are not classics, cannot totally stand apart from the society that produced them. (This
is not to say that they cannot be considered as good literature.) However, it must be remembered that to evaluate them in
terms of twentieth century literary values and conceptualizations of childhood may lead to erroneous conclusions. The importance of these books lies in what they contributed to the
development of children's literature, not in their classic
style or universality in theme. To best understand these late
eighteenth century didactic children's books, it is highly relevant to evaluate them in relationship to the culture that produced them, the contemporary literary trends and traditions
and the prevalent conceptualization of childhood.

It must be remembered that to Mrs. Trimmer, Miss Edgeworth
and the others, didactic literature was not only the proper
form of literature for the child, it was exemplary. To these
didactic writers and to the educational theorists who influenced them, children's literature should teach. There was
little latitude for theme or style in late eighteenth century
children's books. The stories could vary from science lessons
to humanistic concerns, but the end result must, as Mrs. Trimmer wrote, "improve the heart [and] cultivate the understanding."[6] Fantasy and imaginative writing were considered

---

[6]Lance Salway, ed., A Peculiar Gift (Harmondsworth,
Middlesex: Penguin Books, 1976), p. 17.

inappropriate. Locke called it "perfectly useless trumpery." Rousseau demanded that children be given the "naked truth."[7]

Children's literature in the late eighteenth century was seen differently than in our present time. We in the twentieth century see the provision of enjoyment as a primary objective of children's books. In contrast, one mid-eighteenth century didactic writer defined juvenile readings as that which "should inculcate the spirit of geometry in children."[8] Implied is that the books should teach restraint, control and an adherence to externally established rules and axioms. To us this seems an onerous model, but not so to the children's book writers of the late 1700's. It gave them a heroic purpose. They truly believed that by writing in such a way they would "increase the happiness of mankind."[9]

Unabashedly in the prefaces, the selected authors clearly pointed out the morals and purposes of their books. It seemed that they truly wanted recognition for the moral lessons they portrayed, rather than for style, plot, and characterization. They all believed that "early lessons, judiciously given, will prevent the necessity of late lectures."[10] In Fabulous Histories, Mrs. Trimmer urged her young readers to see the stories

---

[7]Townsend, Written for Children, p. 27.

[8]Hazard, Books, Children and Men, p. 12.

[9]Maria Edgeworth, The Parent's Assistant, with a preface by Richard L. Edgeworth (London: R. Hunter, 1822), p. xii.

[10]Maria Edgeworth, Rosamond: A Sequel to Early Lessons (London: R. Hunter, 1821), p. vii.

"as a series of Fables intended to convey a moral instruction applicable to themselves." Richard Edgeworth wrote in the introduction to The Parent's Assistant, "justice, truth, and humanity . . . it is hoped that these principles have never been forgotten in the following pages . . . . It has likewise been attempted in these stories to provide antidotes against ill-humour . . . dissipation, and the fatal propensity to admire and imitate whatever the fashion of the moment may distinguish." Mary Jane Kilner stated in the preface of Jemima Placid, "The main design of this publication is to prove from example, that the pain of disappointment will be much increased by ill-[temper]."

The five selected books, however, are more than just didactic exercises. The authors also knew that for the true lessons of their stories to be absorbed, the books would have to catch and keep the attention of the young. As Richard Edgeworth wrote, "To prevent precepts of morality from tiring the ear and mind, it [is] necessary to make the stories . . . in some measure dramatic; to keep alive hope, and fear, and curiosity."[11] Maria Edgeworth imbued her famous character, Rosamond, with thoughts and behaviors that would be "an image to [the child's] own."[12] These authors strove in their writings "to blend the hints of instruction with the incidents of an

---

[11]Edgeworth, The Parent's Assistant, p. x.

[12]Edgeworth, Rosamond, p. vi.

amusing nature."[13] The former purpose pleased the adult purchaser and critic, the latter captured the attention and accolade of the young. It is perhaps this successful merger that
made these books so well received for so many generations.

The insistence upon the didactic style, and the general
distrust of fantasy, were direct by-products of a world dominated by reason. The pre-industrial and agricultural revolutions produced a large body of new knowledge that would have to
be mastered by the young, particularly those of the middle
classes. This new information would allow them to better function in the increasingly complex world.[14] "Why," wrote Richard
Edgeworth, "should the [child's] mind be filled with fantastic
visions instead of useful knowledge."[15] Besides which, fantasies were considered to arouse the worst passions of man. Passions were seen as potentially causing cleavage from the established church and unrest among the lower classes.

The Age of Reason demanded moderation and constraint--
unrestrained emotions were abhorred and unacceptable. This
tenacious clinging to rationality also gave the adults a very
clear modus operandi in which they could present to the young

---

[13]Mary Ann Kilner, Memoirs of a Peg-Top (London: Marshall,
1782?, reprinted New York: Garland, 1977), p. vi.

[14]Lynne Merle Rosenthal, "The Child Informed: Attitudes
Toward the Socialization in Nineteenth Century English Chil-
dren's Literature" (unpublished Ph.D. dissertation, Columbia
University, 1974), p. 83.

[15]Muriel Jaeger, Before Victoria: Changing Standards and
Behaviors, 1787-1837 (Harmondsworth, Middlesex: Penguin Books,
1956), p. 104.

what they saw as the best of their society. Adults, no matter
what time period they live, desire that their children avoid
their own mistakes and hardships. Late eighteenth century
England was marked by rapid change, confusions, fears. The
adults wanted to give their offspring a more stable world. The
didactic framework was to them the most rational, straightforward way to teach the children the standards and virtues conducive to societal stability.[16]

There may have been another reason for the rise of didacticism and the banishment of sprites, goblins, and pixies from
the nursery. Although this is only conjecture, the authors may
have been aware of the fear provoking quality of the fairy
story, and wished to protect the child reader from it. The
maleficent plans of Snow White's stepmother, the cannibalistic
giant that Jack met, the portentous climb of Sleeping Beauty to
the room housing the fateful spinning wheel--these can be quite
horrifying to a young child. It may also have been the case
that the authors knew of the "reality" of the fairy in the
eighteenth century and wished not to further the image. Fairies then were far more real than today. They were also not
visualized as the diaphanous winged beauties who befriend man,
like Peter Pan's Tinkerbell. Fairies were more wicked, more
fearsome, more quixotic in nature. There was the Bendith y
Maman, who eagerly stole mortal babies and left their own

---

[16]Cornelia Meigs, Elizabeth Nesbitt, Anne T. Eaton, Ruth
Viguers, A Critical History of Children's Literature (New York:
Macmillan, 1967), p. 73.

changelings in their place.[17] One fairy called Black Annes was

"a cannibalistic hag with a blue face and iron claws . . . once

supposed to live in a cave in the Dane Hills in Leicester."[18]

The Red Caps were creatures who lived near the borders between

Scotland and England. They murdered strangers who wandered

into their domain, then dyed their caps in the victim's blood.[19]

With this potentially fearsome nature inherent in the fairy

stories themselves, and the awesomeness of the fairy creatures

that supposedly roamed the English countryside, the five se-

lected authors perhaps wished to rid children's stories of

these elements; thus presenting the young reader with a safer,

more gentle literature.[20]

Didacticism was the major writing style for children's

literature in the eighteenth century. The purposeful teaching

of morals, behaviors and useful information was consistent

---

[17]Katherine Briggs, Abbey Lubbers, Banshees, and Boggarts
(New York: Pantheon, 1979), p. 26.

[18]Ibid., p. 28.

[19]Ibid., p. 131.

[20]One aspect must be brought in here, even though it is
completely contradictory to the authors' purposes in writing
and the societal demands for children's stories. There was an
unconscious infusion of the fairy realm within these didactic
tales. As pointed out before, Jemima Placid could have changed
places with Snow White, et al. Elements of fairy tales were
seen in Evenings at Home. Miss Edgeworth included fairy god-
parents, carefully cloaked in the respectable figure of the
benefector. She even placed a hidden pot of gold in the story
of "The Orphans." Now where could this pot of gold come from?
It could not have been from pirates, for the setting of the
tale took place in the heart of Ireland, not on an island or a
seacoast town. Bandits do not usually stash their stolen riches in pots, rather they use chests or sacks. It is leprechauns
who keep pots of gold hidden about in the Irish countryside.

with an age where reason was king. It mirrored the current
conceptualizations of childhood and child rearing theories. It
also may have accurately reflected the existent parent-child
relationships. Although the documentation found has been
sparse, comments in letters suggest that in actuality, the
child rearing theories were very much in practice and that parents saw one of their main functions as that of a teacher.
Children may have clearly understood that one of their roles
was to patiently listen to adult lectures. The parent-child
relationship in general may have been far more didactic than we
suppose. One example of this can be found in a letter written
by Lord Chesterfield in 1747 to his son. He wasted little time
on niceties and chatter; the entire letter was in truth a lecture on the "art of pleasing." He included very specific rules
such as "Do not tell stories in company," "banish egotism," and
"never maintain an argument." He ended the lesson with the
following sentiment: "These are some of the [secrets] necessary for your initiation in the great society of the world. I
wish I had known them better at your age!"[21] Although sincere
and loving in motivation, this is a very didactic message, far
different from the parent-child interchange of today. However
it is not substantially different from the adult lectures given
in Fabulous Histories, Evenings at Home, the Kilners' books and
Miss Edgeworth's stories.

Letters from children seem also to reflect this more

[21]Douglas Mead, ed., Great English and American Essays
(New York: Rinehart and Co., 1951), pp. 29, 30, 33.

formal parent child relationship. Didacticism seemed to have
been incorporated into the children's lives. On October 9,
1789, an American girl wrote to her mother:

> Honored Madam:
>   Your goodness to me I cannot express. My
> mind is continually crowded with your kindness.
> If your goodness could be rewarded, I hope God
> will repay you. If you remember some time ago, I
> read a story in "The Mothers's Gift" but I hope I
> shall never resemble Miss Gonson. O Dear! What a
> thing it is to disobey one's parents.[22]

A young Quaker boy wrote in December, 1792:

> Dear Father,
>   As I thought thou would be pleased to see my
> writing, I have sent a few lines as a specimen,
> and shall be very glad to hear that thou approves
> there of. I am desirous in learning this and
> every other useful thing, so to improve as to
> gain thy favour and esteem and to show how much I
> am,
>   Thy loving and dutiful son,
>   Jonathan Binns.[23]

These letters suggest that children directly sought their
parents' advice and approval; and that parents were more
straightforward in their advice giving. This fits very neatly
into Locke's conceptualization of childhood and his proposed
child rearing techniques.

The child today is on a more or less equal footing with
the adult generation. He does not tolerate the obviously didactic. The modern child is too sophisticated and is too used
to be involved in decision making processes. But the child of

---

[22]Rosalie Halsey, Forgotten Books of the American Nursery:
A History of the Development of the American Story-Book (Boston: Charles E. Goodspeed, 1911), pp. 113-114.

[23]Rosamond Bayne-Powell, The English Child in the Eighteenth Century (New York: E. P. Dutton, 1939), p. 304.

the eighteenth century was accustomed to a more formal authoritarian relationship with adults, and may have accepted the definition given to him by Locke (and the majority of the middle class parents)--he was an empty vessel to be filled with the proper things. He may not have been delighted with extended lectures given to him by parent or tutor. He may very well have skimmed over the longer moral lessons in his books. He may not, however, have been as aggravated, insulted, or annoyed as one expects our late twentieth century child to be with the didactic lesson.

The major point here is that the conceptualization of the child has changed since the eighteenth century, and will continue to change due to societal pressures, demands, and needs. This conceptualization directly influences education, how parents define their roles and functions, the child's expectations and definitions of himself, and is irrevocably linked with the literature written for the young. When assessing children's literature of any time period, this relationship must be recognized and investigated. When modern critics say that the sternness of historical children's literature results not "from unkindness, but from a starchness, a false perspective, an inflexibility,"[24] it is we in the twentieth century who are being inflexible, not the writers of an earlier era.

Modern critics also seem to forget that both literature for children and the novel form were still in the early stages

---

[24]Hazard, Books, Children and Men, p. 3.

of development in the eighteenth century. Contemporary authors

of books for children have a vast heritage to draw from. They

have the themes and motifs of the oral tradition literature as

well as close to two hundred years of children's books that

have preceded them. The didactic writers under consideration

in this study were not permitted to use the fantasy of the oral

tradition (although as seen, they had unconsciously incorpo-

rated them in their writings) and had few examples of accept-

able children's literature to emulate or from which to gain in-

spiration. Children's literature as we define it had been

begun by Mr. Newbery only some forty years before the selected

women authors began their writing. They were in the forefront

of the development of children's literature, yet they are given

little credit for this today.

The didactic writings are also criticized for not being

equal to the quality of the Newbery publications.[25] It is true

_____

[25]Doris Cole, ed., The Reading of Children: A Symposium
(Syracuse: Syracuse University, 1964), p. 12; W. Boyd Rayward, "What Should They Read? A Historical Perspective," Wilson Library Bulletin (October 1976): 150; Lewis Terman and Margaret Lima, Children's Reading: A Guide for Parents and Teachers (New York: D. Appleton-Century Co., 1931), p. 13. One
reason for this attitude could be that these commentators may
be confusing the late 18th century didactic children's writing
with the "Sunday School" stories that followed at the turn of
the nineteenth century. These Sunday School stories took much
of their structure and organization from the didactic tale but
also inflused in them was a strict evangelical religious fla-
vor. Mrs. Sherwood perhaps is the best known of this group.
Her Fairchild Family and other books contain reactionary, almost Puritanical themes. Mors Moriendum is reintroduced, along
with the concept of the child being innately sinful. The lectures are longer, more pious. The children characters more
strictly controlled by adults. This literature is much different from the writings of Mrs. Trimmer, Mrs. Barbauld, Miss
Edgeworth, and the Kilners, whose works were more gentle, whose

that the late eighteenth century writers included longer and at times more obvious didactic sermons.[26] But it must be recognized that the basic organization, structure, and characters in the didactic stories are quite similar in Newbery's books. If one takes Newbery's most famous children's story, The History of Goody Two Shoes, and compares it to the five didactic books in this study, similarities are striking. Newbery's influence is also quite obvious. Yet it is equally noticeable that the five authors under discussion have gone beyond Newbery in certain respects.

The story of Goody Two Shoes is the tale of a very sweet, docile, honorable, and hard working girl. She is confronted with enormous problems, and through the book overcomes them with her good natured disposition, industrious spirit and virtuous outlook. She is rewarded by being loved and respected by all in the village and eventually marries a fine gentleman. Goody Two Shoes demonstrates many of the weaknesses of the didactic school. The story is told through a succession of basically unlinked events, didactic messages are clearly presented, the characters for the most part are flat, and the story is quite predictable. But at the same time, Mr. Newbery adds drama and suspense, and there is even an episode about "ghosts." The story is, despite its weaknesses, a good one;

---

themes were more universal.

[26]Perhaps this was because the women were sincerely trying to formulate the proper formal habits within their young reader. This was their most important objective. Mr. Newbery, on the other hand, was first and foremost a businessman.

good enough to hold the attention of readers for well over 150
years. (As one young reader said about the book in 1926, "I
like the part where the dog pulled Goody out of school."[27]) In
structure and style, Goody Two Shoes is very similar to the
later didactic writings, but is it really better than them as
some researchers suggest? Not necessarily. In fact, there are
sections in the late eighteenth century didactic stories that
are better. Miss Edgeworth's characterizations and settings
are far superior to those found in Goody Two Shoes. Mrs. Trimmer's interweaving of two stories simultaneously (the Robins
and the Bensons) is a more sophisticated technique than anything found in Newbery's classic. Mrs. Barbauld's and Dr.
Aiken's imagery is more poetic, more innovative. The literary
style in the didactic stories in general is more innovative,
without raising the level of the language above the child's
comprehension. For example, Goody Two Shoes begins as follows:

> All the world must allow that Two Shoes was
> not her real name. No; her Father's Name was
> Meanwell; and he was for years a considerable
> Farmer in the Parish where Margery was born; but
> by Misfortunes which he met with in Business, and
> the wicked Persecutions of Sir Timothy Gripe, and
> an overgrown Farmer named Graspall, he was effec-
> tively ruined.

This is a good introduction. It is succinct, gives the
setting of the story, and introduces the reader to the plight
of Miss Meanwell. It also piques the reader's interest in how
she received the nickname of "Goody Two Shoes." But it

---

[27]Carleton Washburne and Mabel Vogel, What Children Like
to Read: Winnetka Graded Book List (New York: Rand McNally,
1926), p. 91.

does not equal the quality or innovativeness found in the introductions of Fabulous Histories, Jemima Placid, Life and Perambulations of a Mouse, and in the opening paragraphs of some of the stories found in Evenings at Home and The Parent's Assistant. These late eighteenth century authors took the best Newbery had to offer, then refined and expanded it. Although their contribution to children's literature is not as great as John Newbery's, it is substantial and should be recognized.

Not only were Mesdames Barbauld and Trimmer, Maria Edgeworth, and the Kilners working within a whole new genre--literature for children--they were also writing in a new literary form, the novel. Pamela or Virtue Rewarded, written by Richardson in 1740, is considered the first true English novel.[28] Before this date, fictional prose is generally classified as romance, a story told through a "relatively formless succession of events with little consideration of character and motivation."[29] The early English novelists, Richardson, Fielding, Smolett, and Goldsmith changed the form by organizing their episodes and events around a central theme, and by including character development.[30] The novel in its early form, however, is not identical to the twentieth century's conception. For

---

[28] William Thrall and Adison Hibbard, A Handbook to Literature, revised by C. Hugh Holman (New York: Odyssey, 1960), p. 321.

[29] F. E. Halliday, An Illustrated Cultural History of England (New York: Viking Press, 1967), p. 199.

[30] Frederick W. Hillis, ed., The Age of Johnson (New Haven: Yale University Press, 1949), p. 114.

one thing the modern novelist expects and desires that the reader become "captive inside the covers."[31] He attempts to create his characters to stand alone, to be self-explanatory in word and action. This was not the case with the eighteenth century novelist. He felt it was his duty to interject comments and lectures on human conduct. The characters were often used to lay the groundwork and set the stage for the authors' digressions, rather than to speak for themselves. Moral edification was the eighteenth century novelist's objective, his aphorisms helped to obtain this goal.[32] These moral digressions also served another function. The new novelists in the 1700's were not totally clear and comfortable in this new form. The purposes, methods, and limitations of the novel were still ill defined. The didactic interruptions helped give a legitimacy to this new form, for both the author and the reading public.[33]

When modern historians criticize the didacticism of the selected books, claiming that it breaks narrative flow, destroys characterization, and weakens the plot, they are not considering other eighteenth century writings. Richardson is not criticized for his didacticism. It is understood by the critics that his genius lay in helping to create a new literary

---

[31]James L. Clifford, ed., Man Versus Society in Eighteenth Century Britain: Six Points of View (Cambridge: Cambridge University Press, 1968), p. 130.

[32]Hillis, The Age of Johnson, p. 114.

[33]Ibid., p. 116.

style. The didactic quality of his books was necessary. It was, in part, the way he defined the novel. Newbery is rarely accused of being didactic. Rather he is lauded for his innovativeness, the natural appeal and the quality that he brought to children's literature. Yet when modern commentators review the authors selected for this study--women who were writing just forty years later than Newbery and Richardson--they are referred to as the "Monstrous Regiment," puritanical, and far removed from children's interests and needs. Modern critics "too often forget how genuine was their motive . . . in attempting to create literature in a new medium . . . [and] that they broke ground for [other] . . . writers who were to come."[34] When modern commentators pull this late eighteenth century literature out of its time period, disregarding contemporary child rearing practices, conceptualizations of childhood, and literary traditions, their evaluations tend to be unduly harsh.

Another factor that may be causing the discrepancy between the criticisms included in this study and those in traditional histories is that some commentators may be forgetting the importance of moral literature in the development of children. In 1892, Felix Adler wrote that moral literature is exceedingly important for children, for it acts as "a glass in which we see our best selves reflected." He then went on to tell a legend about two spirits:

---

[34]Meigs, A Critical History of Children's Literature, p. 73.

> The one an angel, the other a demon, that accompany every human being through life and walk invisibly at his side. The one represents our bad self, the other our better self.

To Mr. Adler the important moral service which good literature gives its reader is to make "the invisible angel visible."[35] The characters of Jemima Placid, the Benson children, Jem, Francesco, Simple Susan and the others do just this. They represent the best human qualities to the readers. The villains in the stories clearly show the worst. The didactic authors then go further by reassuring the child that this "invisible angel" will indeed emerge, if he puts forth the effort and thought.

In this century Bruno Bettelheim has reiterated much of Mr. Adler's hypothesis on the importance of clear, moralistic literature.[36] Bettelheim maintains that in the early development of the personality, the child needs clear models to emulate. The young child sees things in extremes, the polarities of the situation are understood, not the grayish middle ground. This ambivalency of life "must wait until a relatively firm personality has been established on the basis of positive identifications . . . . The more simple and straightforward a good character, the easier for the child to identify with it, and reject the bad one."[37] It is Dr. Bettelheim's contention that

---

[35] Felix Adler, The Moral Education of Children (New York: D. Appleton, 1908), p. 32.

[36] It is interesting to note that both Adler and Bettelheim feel that the fairy tale is the perfect moral literature for the young.

[37] Bruno Bettelheim, The Uses of Enchantment (New York:

much of the child-appeal and psychological importance of the
fairy-folk story lies in the clear presentation of right tri-
umphing over evil, the good character versus the bad. This
quality is consistently seen in the late eighteenth century
didactic story as well. Good always defeats evil. The good
characters are always rewarded, the bad ones punished. With
the exception of some of the character development seen in Miss
Edgeworth's tales and Fabulous Histories, the majority of the
characters are exceedingly one sided, being very very good or
very very bad, exactly like those characters seen in the fairy
tale. These flat characters are not sophisticated, are not
thought provoking, they are not realistic. Their appeal lies
in fulfilling the child's need for heroic role models and for
showing a clear distinction between good and evil. Critics may
say that the didactic ignores the child's needs and interests.
On the contrary, it may fulfill the child's psychological needs
as successfully as the fairy tale.

Perhaps it is time for scholars to re-evaluate and re-
examine the concept of didacticism in children's literature.
To discredit stories written for children because they are
didactic seems not only unjust but it may also indicate a major
misconception of the literary genre itself. Mr. Adler and
Dr. Bettelheim hypothesized that much of which is so character-
istic of the didactic style is psychologically beneficial for
the child. Scholars such as Plumb, Rosenthal, Avery, and

_____

Alfred A. Knopf, 1976), pp. 9-10.

Hentoff suggest that children's literature, by its very nature (i.e., stories for the younger members of society) is a teaching tool; a device to teach societal expectations, ideals, and mores. These societal goals and expectations are presented to help the child learn to be a moral and productive adult within the society.

Mr. Townsend wrote that in truth didactic literature is as present in modern children's books as it was in the eighteenth century stories. "It is hard to avoid the conclusion that Didacticism is still very much alive and that by an engaging intellectual frailty, we are able to reject the concept while accepting the reality."[38] The major difference between eighteenth century and twentieth century didacticism is perhaps that the modern writer is more skilled, thus more subtle and sophisticated in his presentation. In reviewing children's literature, it therefore seems important to recognize both the didactic quality of the literature and the societal and philosophical forces determining what teachings should be included.

Therefore, it is significant to study early children's literature, not to just criticize it. The importance of these early examples lies not in what makes or does not make them "great literature" but rather what makes them milestones in the development of the genre. By understanding this early literature in light of the historical-social trends that formed

---

[38]Shiela Egoff, G. T. Stubbs, and L. F. Ashley, ed., _Only Connect: Readings on Children's Literature_ (New York: Oxford University, 1969), p. 34.

them--the prevalent conceptualization of childhood, child rearing practices, and educational philosophies; we can better understand and critique our modern children's literature and the forces from whence they emerge.

THE BOOK

(Anonymous, 1815)

My pretty child I am your friend,
    And much to me you owe;
'Til I to you some knowledge lend,
    How little do you know!

I am a book for girls or boys,
    To tell them this or that;
I never din them with my noise,
    Or teaze them with my chat.

For if you think you have enough
    Of my good company,
To put me by, I take no huff,
    But pray be kind unto me.

O do not turn my corners down!
    Tho' little dogs have ears,
As I'm a book of high renown,
    Affront me not my dears.

My page a bosom never grieves,
    Nor wounds your heart with pain;
Then do not tear my tender leaves,
    Nor back my cover stain.

Altho' I'm drest in plain attire,
    Yet look upon my face:
My chearful features you'll admire;
    For they are marked with grace.

Now shut me up, and put me by,
    And rest your little brain;
And where I'm put I'll quiet lie,
    Till you shall read again.

                    from Little Poems
                    for Children, pp.
                    21-22.

A SELECTED BIBLIOGRAPHY

"A Forgotten Children's Book." Hibbert Magazine, Autumn 1964, pp. 27-34.

Adler, Felix. The Moral Education of Children. New York: D. Appleton, 1908.

Aiken, Dr. John, and Barbauld, Mrs. Evenings at Home. London: George Routledge and Sons, n.d.

Allibone, Austin S. A Critical Dictionary of English Literature: British and American Authors, Vol. I. Philadelphia: J. B. Lippincott, 1870.

Altick, Richard, The English Common Reader: A Social History of the Mass Reading Public, 1800-1900. Chicago: University of Chicago Press, 1957.

Andreae, Gesiena. The Dawn of Juvenile Literature in England. Amsterdam: H. J. Paris, 1925.

Aries, Philippe. Centuries of Childhood. New York: Alfred A. Knopf, 1962.

Avery, Gillian. Nineteenth Century Children: Heroes and Heroines in English Children's Stories, 1780-1900. London: Hodder and Stoughton, 1965.

Barbauld, Mrs. Hymns in Prose for Children. Edinburgh: Oliver and Boyd, 1830.

Barry, Florence. A Century of Children's Books. London: Methuen and Co., 1922.

Bayne-Powell, Rosamond. The English Child in the Eighteenth Century. New York: E. P. Dutton and Co., 1939.

Belloc, Hillaire. "Children's Books." Living Age 276 (January 18, 1913): 186-189.

Bettelheim, Bruno. The Uses of Enchantment. New York: Alfred A. Knopf, 1976.

Beust, Nora, ed. Graded List of Books for Children. Chicago: American Library Association, 1930.

Boreman, Thomas. The Gigantick History of Two Famous Giants and Other Curiosities in Guildhall. London, 1740-1743. reprint ed., New York: Garland Publishers, 1977.

Briggs, Asa. The Age of Improvement. London: Longmans, Green and Co., 1959.

Briggs, Katherine. Abbey Lubbers, Banshees and Boggarts. New York: Pantheon, 1979.

Butler, Francelia, ed. Children's Literature. Vol. 10. New Haven: Yale University, 1981.

Children's Literature, Vol. I. Philadelphia: Temple University Press, 1972.

Clarke, Isabel C. Maria Edgeworth: Her Family and Friends. London: Hutchinson and Co., n.d.

Clifford, James L., ed. Man Versus Society in Eighteenth-Century Britain: Six Points of View. Cambridge: Cambridge University Press, 1968.

Cole, Doris M., ed. The Reading of Children: A Symposium. Syracuse: Syracuse University, 1964.

Cruse, Amy. The Englishman and His Books in the Early Nineteenth Century. New York: Benjamin Blom, 1968.

Cullinan, Bernice E. Literature and the Child. New York: Harcourt, Brace, Jovanovich, 1981.

Dalgliesh, Alice. First Experiences with Literature. New York: Charles Scribner's Sons, 1932.

Darton, F. J. Harvey. Children's Books in England: Five Centuries of Social Life. Cambridge: Cambridge University, 1958.

Dickenson, Peter. "The Day of the Rabbit," The Quarterly Journal of the Library of Congress 38 (Fall 1981): 203-219.

Dobson, Austin. "The Parent's Assistant," DeLibris: Prose and Verse. London: Macmillan, 1911; reprinted in Signal 17 (May 1975): 96-104.

Downs, Brian W. Richardson. London: George Routledge, 1928.

"Edgeworth Family: Anticipators of Froebel." New York Times, educational supp., May 27, 1949, p. 335.

Edgeworth, Maria. Castle Rackrent and the Absentee, introduction by Brendes Matthews. London: J. M. Dent, n.d.

_____. The Parent's Assistant, 6 Vols., introduction by Richard Lovell Edgeworth. London: Baldwin, Cradock and Joy, 1822.

_____. Rosamond: A Sequel to Early Lessons. London: R. Hunter, 1821.

Egoff, Shiela; Stubbs, G. T.; and Ashley, L. F., ed. Only Connect: Readings on Children's Literature. New York: Oxford University, 1969.

Ellis, Alec. How to Find Out About Children's Literature. Oxford: Pergamon Press, 1966.

Ellis, Mrs. The Wives of England: Their Relative Duties, Influence, and Social Obligations. New York: D. Appleton, 1843.

Elwood, Anne Katherine. Memoirs of the Literary Ladies of England, Vol. I. London: Henry Colburn, 1843. reprinted, New York: AMS Press, n.d.

Fader, Daniel, and Bornstein, George. British Periodicals of the Eighteenth and Nineteenth Centuries. Ann Arbor: University Microfilms, 1972.

Fenwick, Sara Innis, ed. A Critical Approach to Children's Literature. Chicago: University of Chicago, 1967.

Field, Elinor, ed. Hornbook Reflections: 1949-1966. Boston: The Horn Book, 1969.

Field, Mrs. The Child and His Book. London: Wells Gardner, Darton and Co., 1892.

Gillespie, Margaret. Literature for Children: History and Trends. Dubuque, Iowa: William C. Brown, 1970.

Gloag, John, and Thompson, Walter C. Home Life in History: Social Life and Manners in Britain, 200 B.C.-1926 A.D. New York: Benjamin Blom, 1972.

Green, Roger Lancelyn. Tellers of Tales. New York: Franklin Watts, 1965.

Greenleaf, Barbara Kaye. Children Through the Ages. New York: McGraw-Hill, 1978.

Halliday, F. E. An Illustrated Cultural History of England. New York: Viking Press, 1967.

Halsey, Rosalie. Forgotten Books of the American Nursery: A History of the Development of the American Story-Book. Boston: Charles E. Goodspeed and Co., 1911.

Hamilton, Catherine J. Women Writers: Their Works and Ways. 1st Series, 1892. reprint ed., Freeport, New York: Books for Libraries Press, 1971.

Harrison, Barbara. "Why Study Children's Literature?" The Quarterly Journal of the Library of Congress 38 (Fall 1981): 243-253.

Haviland, Virginia, ed. Children's Literature: Views and Reviews. New York: Lothrop, Lee & Shepard, 1973.

Hazard, Paul. Books, Children, and Men. Boston: The Horn Book, 1947.

Hewins, Caroline. "The History of Children's Books." Atlantic Monthly, January 1888, pp. 112-126.

Hillis, Frederick W., ed. The Age of Johnson. New Haven: Yale University Press, 1949.

Hole, Christina. English Home Life: 1500-1800. London: B. T. Batsford, Ltd., 1947.

Hunt, Clara. What Shall We Read to the Children? Boston: Houghton Mifflin, 1915.

Hunt, D. "The Historical Background: Philippe Aries and the Evolution of the Family," from a collection of articles gathered for a course at Ben Gurion University, Beer Sheva, Israel, 1978.

Jaeger, Muriel. Before Victoria: Changing Standards and Behaviors, 1787-1837. Harmondsworth, Middlesex: Penguin Books, 1956.

James, Philip. English Book Illustration: 1800-1900. New York: Penguin Books, 1947.

Jan, Isabelle. On Children's Literature. London: Bayles and Sons, 1973.

Kiefer, Monica. American Children through their Books: 1700-1835. Philadelphia: University of Pennsylvania Press, 1948.

Kilner, Dorothy. The Life and Perambulations of a Mouse. Philadelphia: Lippincott, 1849.

Kilner, Mary Ann. Memoirs of a Peg-Top. London: John Marshall, 1782? reprint ed., New York: Garland, 1977.

_____. Jemima Placid. London: Marshall, 1793(?).

Law, Alice. "The Cult of the Child-Spirit in Modern Literature." Transactions of the Royal Society of Literature of the United Kingdom, second series, Vol. XXXIII, 1915. reprint ed., Kraus Reprint, 1970, pp. 118-142.

Little Poems for Children. Windsor, Vt.: Jesse Cochran, 1815.

Madison, Charles. *Book Publishing in America*. New York: McGraw-Hill, 1968.

Mahoney, Bertha E., ed. *Realms of Gold in Children's Books*. New York: Doubleday, Dorant and Co., 1929.

Marshall, Dorothy. *Eighteenth-Century England*. New York: David McKay Co., 1962.

Mause, Lloyd de, ed. *The History of Childhood*. New York: Psychohistory Press, 1974.

Mead, Douglas, ed. *Great English and American Essays*. New York: Rinehart and Co., 1951.

Meigs, Cornelia; Nesbitt, Elizabeth; Eaton, Anne T.; and Viguers, Ruth. *A Critical History of Children's Literature*. New York: Macmillan, 1967.

Moore, Anne Carroll. *My Roads to Childhood: Views and Reviews of Children's Literature*. Boston: The Horn Book, 1918.

Moore, Annie E. *Literature Old and New for Children*. Cambridge, Massachusetts: Houghton Mifflin, 1934.

_____. "The Reviewing of Children's Books." *Bookman* 61 (May 1925): 325-331.

Morgan, R. B., ed. *Reading in English Social History*. Cambridge: Cambridge University Press, 1923.

Moses, Montrose. *Children's Books and Reading*. New York: Mitchell Kennerly, 1907.

_____. "Convalescent Children's Literature." *North American Review* 221 (April 1925): 528-539.

Muir, Percy. *English Children's Books from 1600-1900*. New York: Frederick A. Praeger, 1954.

_____. *Victorian Illustrated Books*. New York: Praeger, 1971.

Mumby, Frank A. *Publishing and Bookselling*. London: Jonathan Cape, 1956.

Newby, P. H. *Maria Edgeworth*. Denver: Allen Swallow, 1950.

Oliver, Grace A. *A Study of Maria Edgeworth*. Boston: A. Williams and Co., 1882.

Opie, Peter. "John Newbery and His Successors." Book Collector 24 (Summer 1975): 259-269.

"The Parent's Assistant by Maria Edgeworth: A Review." The Monthly Review 21 (Spetember 1796): 89.

Paterson, Katherine. "Sounds in the Heart." Horn Book, December 1981, pp. 694-702.

Patterson, Sylvia W. Rousseau's Emile and Early Children's Literature. Metuchen, New Jersey: Scarecrow Press, 1971.

Plumb, J. H. England in the Eighteenth Century: 1714-1815. Harmondsworth, Middlesex: Penguin Books, 1950.

_____. Foreword to Early Children's Books and their Illustration: Pierpont-Morgan Library, by Gerald Gottlieb. Boston: David R. Godine, 1975.

_____. "The New World of Children in Eighteenth-Century England." Past and Present 67 (1975): 64-93.

Pollard, M. "Maria Edgeworth's The Parent's Assistant, the First Edition," Book Collector 20 (Autumn 1971): 345-351.

Quale, Eric. The Collector's Book of Children's Books. New York: Clarkson N. Potter, 1971.

Quinlin, Maurice J. Victorian Prelude: A History of English Manners, 1700-1830. Hamden, Connecticut: Archon Books, 1965.

Rayward, W. Boyd. "What Shall They Read: A Historical Perspective." Wilson Library Bulletin, October 1976, pp. 146-153.

Repplier, Agnes. A Happy Half Century and Other Essays. Boston: Houghton Mifflin, 1908.

Rigby, Elizabeth. "Books for Children." Quarterly Review 71 (1844): 54-83.

Robinson, Evelyn. Readings About Children's Literature. New York: David McKay, 1966.

Rodgers, Betsey. Georgian Chronicle: Mrs. Barbauld and Her Family. London: Methuen and Co., 1958.

Roscoe, S. John Newbery and His Successors: A Bibliography. Wormley, Hertfordshire: Five Owls Press, 1973.

Rosenthal, Lynne Merle. "The Child Informed: Attitudes Toward the Socialization of the Child in the Nineteenth-Century English Children's Literature." Ph.D. dissertation, Columbia University, 1974.

Saint John, Judith, ed. The Osbourne Collection of Early Children's Books: 1566-1910. Toronto: Toronto Public Library, 1958.

_____. "Mrs. Trimmer--Guardian of Education." Hornbook, February 1970, pp. 20-25.

Salway, Lance, ed. A Peculiar Gift. Harmondsworth, Middlesex: Penguin Books, 1976.

Smith, Elva S. The History of Children's Literature, revised by Margaret Hodges and Susan Steinfirst. Chicago: American Library Association, 1980.

Smith, James Steele. A Critical Approach to Children's Literature. New York: McGraw-Hill, 1967.

Smith, Janet Adam. Children's Illustrated Books. London: Collins, 1958.

Smith, Lillian. The Unreluctant Years. New York: Viking Press, 1953.

Snoden, David. A Mighty Ferment: Britain in the Age of Revolution, 1750-1850. New York: The Seabury Press, 1978.

Some Account of the Life and Writings of Mrs. Trimmer. 2 Vol. London: F. C. and J. Rivington, 1814.

Stone, Lawrence. The Family, Sex and Marriage in England: 1500-1800. New York: Harper and Row, 1979.

Targ, William, ed. Bibliophile in the Nursery. New York: The World Publishing Co., 1957.

Terman, Lewis M., and Lima, Margaret. Children's Reading: A Guide for Parents and Teachers. New York: D. Appleton-Century Co., 1931.

Thrall, William, and Hibbard, Addison. A Handbook to Literature, revised by C. Hugh Holman. New York: Odyssey, 1960.

Thwaite, Mary. From Primer to Pleasure in Reading. Boston: Horn Book, 1963.

Titmarsh, Michael Angelo (William Thackeray). "On Some Illustrated Books." Fraser's Magazine, April 1846, pp. 495-502.

Townsend, John Rowe. Written for Children: An Outline of English Children's Literature. Philadelphia: Lippincott, 1974.

Trimmer, Mrs. A Description of a Set of Prints of Ancient History. 2 Vol. London: Baldwin, Cradock and Joy, 1821.

_____. Fabulous Histories. London: Scott, Webster and Geary, 1840.

_____. The Guardian of Education. 5 Vol. London: J. Hatchard, 1802-1806.

Turberville, A. S. English Men and Manners in the Eighteenth Century. Oxford: Clarendon Press, 1932.

Washburne, Carleton, and Vogel, Mabel. What Children Like to Read: Winnetka Graded Book List. New York: Rand McNally, 1926.

Weekes, Blanche E. Literature and the Child. New York: Silver Burdett Company, 1935.

Welsh, Charles. "Some Notes on the History of Books for Children, 1800-1850." Newbery House Magazine, August 1890, pp. 85-92.

_____. "The Children's Books That Have Lived." The Library. NSI 1900: 314-323.

White, Gleason. Children's Books and Their Illustrators. The Studio (Monograph). Special Winter Number 1897-1898.

Yarde, D. M. The Life and Works of Sarah Trimmer. The Hounslow District Historical Society, 1972.

Yonge, Miss. "Children's Literature of the Last Century." Macmillan Magazine, July 1869, pp. 229-237.